The World
Environment
& The Global Economy

IDEAS in CONFLICT

Marnie McCuen

publications inc.

411 Mallalieu Drive
Hudson, Wisconsin 54016
Phone (715) 386-7113

Illustration and Photo Credits

Bruce Beattie 37; David Catrow 80; Henry Payne 73; Joe Pett 144; Mike Ritter 17; Andrew Singer 128.

© 1999 by Gary E. McCuen Publications, Inc.
411 Mallalieu Drive, Hudson, Wisconsin 54016

(715) 386-7113

International Standard Book Number
0-86596-179-4
Printed in the United States of America

CONTENTS

Ideas in Conflict

Chapter 1   CLIMATE CHANGE

Chapter 2   WORLD ENVIRONMENT: UNDER CONTROL OR UNDER SIEGE?

Chapter 3   **ENVIRONMENT, ECONOMY, AND
ETHICS: IDEAS IN CONFLICT**

REASONING SKILL DEVELOPMENT

These activities may be used as individualized study guides for students in libraries and resource centers or as discussion catalysts in small group and classroom discussions.

IDEAS in CONFLICT

This series features ideas in conflict on political, social, and moral issues. It presents counterpoints, debates, opinions, commentary, and analysis for use in libraries and classrooms. Each title in the series uses one or more of the following basic elements:

Introductions that present an issue overview giving historic background and/or a description of the controversy.

Counterpoints and debates carefully chosen from publications, books, and position papers on the political right and left to help librarians and teachers respond to requests that treatment of public issues be fair and balanced.

Symposiums and forums that go beyond debates that can polarize and oversimplify. These present commentary from across the political spectrum that reflect how complex issues attract many shades of opinion.

A *global* emphasis with foreign perspectives and surveys on various moral questions and political issues that will help readers to place subject matter in a less culture-bound and ethnocentric frame of reference. In an ever-shrinking and interdependent world, understanding and cooperation are essential. Many issues are global in nature and can be effectively dealt with only by common efforts and international understanding.

Reasoning skill study guides and discussion activities provide ready-made tools for helping with critical reading and evaluation of content. The guides and activities deal with one or more of the following:

RECOGNIZING AUTHOR'S POINT OF VIEW

INTERPRETING EDITORIAL CARTOONS

VALUES IN CONFLICT

WHAT IS EDITORIAL BIAS?

WHAT IS SEX BIAS?

WHAT IS POLITICAL BIAS?

WHAT IS ETHNOCENTRIC BIAS?

WHAT IS RACE BIAS?

WHAT IS RELIGIOUS BIAS?

*From across **the political spectrum** varied sources are presented for research projects and classroom discussions. Diverse opinions in the series come from magazines, newspapers, syndicated columnists, books, political speeches, foreign nations, and position papers by corporations and nonprofit institutions.*

About the Publisher

The late Gary E. McCuen was an editor and publisher of anthologies for libraries and discussion materials for schools and colleges. His publications have specialized in social, moral and political conflict. They include books, pamphlets, cassettes, tabloids, filmstrips and simulation games, most of them created from his many years of experience in teaching and educational publishing.

CHAPTER 1

CLIMATE CHANGE

THE DARK SIDE OF GLOBAL WARMING

Daniel Becker

Daniel Becker is Director of the Sierra Club Global Warming and Energy Program. The Sierra Club is a nonprofit, member-supported, public interest organization that promotes conservation of the natural environment by influencing public policy decisions on the administrative, legislative, legal and electoral levels. Sierra Club, 85 Second St., Second Floor, San Francisco, CA 94105-3441, USA, phone: (415) 977-5500, fax: (415) 977-5799, www.sierraclub.org.

■ POINTS TO CONSIDER

1. Summarize the meaning of the term "global warming." What does the Sierra Club credit for global warming?

2. What damage to the physical environment will result from global warming, according to Becker?

3. What threats to human health will result from global warming, according to the author?

4. Discuss the author's suggestions for ending the warming trend. How will these policy recommendations affect the economy?

Excerpted from the testimony of Daniel Becker before the U.S. House Committee on International Relations, July 24, 1997.

Man-made global warming is occurring much faster; faster in fact than at any other time in human history.

The human race is engaged in the largest and most dangerous experiment in history – an experiment to see what will happen to our health and the health of the planet when we make drastic changes to our climate. This is not part of some deliberate scientific inquiry. It is an uncontrolled experiment on the Earth, and we are gambling our children's future on its outcome.

GLOBAL WARMING

The rapid buildup of carbon dioxide and other "greenhouse gases" in our atmosphere is the source of the problem. Over the last one hundred years we have increased the concentrations of key global warming pollutants in our atmosphere. For example, carbon dioxide (CO_2), the primary global warming gas, has increased by 30%. By burning ever-increasing quantities of coal, oil, and gas we are literally changing the atmosphere.

The results of global warming pollution are already significant. Many regions of the world have warmed by as much as five degrees Fahrenheit. Physicians at Harvard and Johns Hopkins Medical Schools and other medical institutions have issued grim assessments that global warming may already be causing the spread of infectious diseases and increasing heat wave deaths. Increased flooding, storms, and agricultural losses could devastate our economy. Sea level rise threatens to inundate one third of Florida and Louisiana and entire island nations. If we do not curb global warming pollution, our children and grandchildren will live in a world with a climate far less hospitable than today.

LEADING CLIMATE SCIENTISTS

More than 2500 of the world's leading climate scientists, participating in the United Nations-sponsored Intergovernmental Panel on Climate Change (IPCC) examined evidence. They have concluded that "the balance of evidence suggests a discernible human influence on global climate."

The IPCC scientists project that during our children's and grandchildren's lifetimes global warming will raise the world's average temperature by two to six degrees Fahrenheit. By comparison, the Earth is only five to nine degrees Fahrenheit warmer today than it was 10,000 years ago during the last ice age.

Throughout history, major shifts in temperature have occurred at a rate of a few degrees over thousands of years. They were accompanied by radical changes, including the extinction of many species. Man-made global warming is occurring much faster; faster in fact than at any other time in human history.

Unless we slow and ultimately reverse the buildup of greenhouse gases, we will have only decades, not millennia, to try to adapt to major changes in weather patterns, sea levels, and serious threats to human health. Plants and animals that cannot adapt to the new conditions will become extinct.

THREATS TO HUMAN HEALTH

Both the IPCC and the World Health Organization project that more frequent and more severe heat waves will be an early effect of global warming. The deadly stretch of hot days that combined with record night time heat to kill more than 700 people in Chicago during the summer of 1995 is the type of event that scientists project will become more common. National Oceanic and Atmospheric Administration's (NOAA) National Climactic Data Center has already documented that the number and intensity of extreme weather events, such as heat waves, are increasing.

Infectious disease is the second major threat that global warming poses to human health. As temperatures rise, disease-carrying mosquitoes and rodents move into new areas, infecting people in their wake. Scientists at the Harvard Medical School have linked recent U.S. outbreaks of dengue ("breakbone") fever, malaria, hantavirus and other diseases to climate change.

In 1995, when McAllen, Texas, suffered an outbreak of dengue fever, the *Houston Chronicle's* headline read, "Warming Climate Invites Dengue Fever to Texas." Scientists reported that an unusually mild winter and hotter than normal summer contributed to the spread of the mosquito-borne disease.

Outbreaks of encephalitis, another mosquito-borne illness with strong links to warmer temperatures, also appear to be on the rise. Since 1987 there have been outbreaks in Arizona, California, Colorado, Florida, Louisiana, Mississippi, and Texas.

Global warming may also mean millions more people around the world will become infected with malaria. The spread of the malaria-carrying mosquito is limited by cold temperatures. As warmer temperatures spread north and south from the tropics, and to higher elevations, malaria-carrying mosquitoes will spread with them. IPCC scientists conclude that global warming will likely put as much as 65% of the world's population at risk of infection – an increase of 20%.

Here in the U.S., Houston has experienced a malaria outbreak in each of the last two years. In the 1990s malaria cases have occurred as far north as New Jersey, Michigan and New York.

The serious health threats global warming poses caused the World Health Organization to conclude that a "wait-and-see approach would be imprudent at best and nonsensical at worst."

OUR COASTS

Rising seas threaten low-lying areas of the United States. Global warming contributes to sea level rise in two ways.

First, as glaciers and other land ice melts, the water flows to the oceans adding to its volume. Climate models, which the IPCC studied, predict greater warming at higher altitudes and at the poles. Scientists are now observing these predictions, providing more disturbing signs that global warming has begun. Over the last 100 years, the world's glaciers have shrunk by about 11%; about 50% of glaciers in the Alps have melted away.

Second, as temperatures rise, the volume of the water expands, just as the volume of the liquid in a thermometer rises with temperature. Unlike a thermometer, of course, our coasts are not always high enough to prevent the rising seas from flooding the land.

Sea levels have already risen an average of four to ten inches over the last 100 years. The IPCC projects that sea levels will rise a further two feet over the next 100 years. Higher sea levels will combine with more powerful storms and the results could be devastating. Huge portions – as much as one third – of low-lying states, such as Louisiana and Florida, are at risk of flooding. Frank Nutter of the Reinsurance Institute of America has noted that climate change has already raised property insurance rates in Florida in areas particularly at risk of sea level rise.

THE CULPRITS: FOSSIL FUELS

Global warming is a pollution problem. Gas-guzzling cars and light trucks such as mini-vans and sport utility vehicles are major sources of this pollution. Over its lifetime, the average vehicle on the road today will spew about 50 tons of CO_2 pollution into the air. Raising fuel economy standards to 45 miles per gallon (mpg) would cut that by more than half, to 23 tons.

Global warming pollution also comes from the burning of coal, oil, and to a lesser extent, natural gas in our power plants. Coal is especially "dirty," producing nearly twice as much CO_2 per unit of heat produced as natural gas, and a third more than oil.

Deforestation also contributes to global warming. Trees "breathe in" CO_2 and can work to remove part of the pollution we release from the air. When trees are cut down or burned, however, they release carbon dioxide back into the air. The burning of massive areas of forest for farming in the Amazon, Asia and other areas of the world releases enormously large quantities of carbon dioxide into the atmosphere.

SOLUTIONS

The good news is we can curb and eventually stop global warming, but we must begin to act now. We can do this while strengthening the U.S. economy and creating jobs.

The key to curbing global warming is improving energy efficiency. Our cars and light trucks, homes, and power plants could be made much more efficient by simply installing the best current technology. Energy efficiency is the cleanest, safest, most cost-effective way we can begin to deal with global warming.

As much CO_2 spews from the tailpipes of America's cars and light trucks as from all sources in the entire nation of Japan. The single biggest step we can take to curb global warming is to make our cars and sport utilities go further on a gallon of gas by raising Corporate Average Fuel Economy (CAFE) standards to 45 mpg for cars and 34 for light trucks. This will cut U.S. emissions by 140 million metric tons.

Higher CAFE standards will also save three million barrels of oil daily, cut our dangerous dependence on Organization of Petroleum Exporting Countries (OPEC) oil, curb our trade deficits (one third of which goes for oil), cut urban smog, and save consumers money at the pump.

We also need to clean up our electric power plants. Most electric utilities still use coal to produce electricity, spewing millions of tons of CO_2 and other pollution into the atmosphere every year. Part of the problem could be solved by converting these plants to burn cleaner natural gas. We could do much more to save energy in our homes and office buildings. More energy efficient lighting, heating and air-conditioning could keep millions of tons of CO_2 out of our air each year.

Harnessing the clean, abundant energy of the sun and wind is critical to solving the global warming problem. Technological advances have brought the cost of electricity generated by the wind down by 85% since 1981. Solar energy technology has made remarkable progress as new photovoltaic cells have been developed to convert ever greater amounts of sunlight directly into electricity. Today the costs of wind and solar power are approaching that of cheap, dirty coal plants.

CONCLUSION

We must also recognize that inaction has high costs. If we fail to act to curb global warming we will impose on our children enormous impacts on health, coasts, agriculture, and infrastructure. These impacts carry a price tag in the hundreds of billions of dollars. And, what is the dollar value on lives lost to heat waves, infectious disease, and extreme weather?

READING

2

THE SUNNY SIDE OF GLOBAL WARMING

Dennis T. Avery

Dennis T. Avery is Director of the Center for Global Food Issues, a project of the Hudson Institute. He is editor for Global Food Quarterly *and author of a book about saving wildlife with high-yield farming,* Saving the Planet with Pesticides and Plastic: The Environmental Triumph of High Yield Farming.

■ POINTS TO CONSIDER

1. Describe the "Little Climate Optimum." Why does this period give the author reason for optimism about global warming?

2. Examine the benefits of global warming, according to the reading. What regions and peoples would receive these benefits?

3. Why does the author discount the arguments of environmental activists? Give one such argument and the author's response.

4. What are the "costs" of reducing greenhouse gases, according to Avery?

Excerpted from Avery, Dennis T. "Global Warming – Boon for Mankind?" **American Outlook** of the Hudson Institute. Spring 1998: 12-6. Reprinted by permission, Hudson Institute.

If there is any global warming in the twenty-first century, it will produce the kind of milder, more-pleasant weather that marked the Medieval Little Optimum.

...Between 900 AD and 1300 AD, the earth warmed by some four to seven degrees Fahrenheit – almost exactly what the models now predict for the twenty-first century. History books call it the Little Climate Optimum. Written and oral history tells us that the warming created one of the most favorable periods in human history. Crops were plentiful, death rates diminished, and trade and industry expanded – while art and architecture flourished.

MEDIEVAL GLOBAL WARMING

The world's population experienced far less hunger. Food production surged because winters were milder and growing seasons longer. Key growing regions had fewer floods and droughts. Human death rates declined, partly because of the decrease in hunger and partly because people spent less of their time huddled in damp, smoke-filled hovels that encouraged the growth and spread of tuberculosis and other infectious diseases.

Prosperity, fostered by the abundant crops and lower death rates, stimulated a huge outpouring of human creativity – in engineering, trade, architecture, religion, art, and practical invention.

Soon after the year 1400, however, the good weather ended. The world dropped into the Little Ice Age, with harsher cold, fiercer storms, severe droughts, more crop failures, and more famines. According to climate historian H.H. Lamb, during this period, "for much of the [European] continent, the poor were reduced to eating dogs, cats, and even children." The cold trend persisted until the 18th century....

AGRICULTURAL BONANZA

The medieval experience with global warming should reassure us greatly, and the latest scientific evidence supports such optimism. It is clear, for example, that a planet earth with longer growing seasons, more rainfall, and higher carbon dioxide levels would be a "plant heaven." Modest warming would help crops, not hinder them....

Cartoon by Mike Ritter. Reprinted with permission, **King Feature Syndicate.**

The expected increase in CO_2 will be an additional blessing. Carbon dioxide acts like fertilizer for plants. Dutch greenhouses, for example, routinely and deliberately triple their CO_2 levels – and the crops respond with 20 to 40 percent yield increases. Extra CO_2 also helps plants use their water more efficiently. The "pores" (stomata) on plant leaves partially close, and less water vapor escapes from inside the plants. More than a thousand experiments with 475 crop plant varieties in 29 separate countries show that doubling the world's carbon dioxide would raise crop yields an average of 52 percent....

LUSH FORESTS AND PRAIRIES

The increase in CO_2 will make forests all over the world healthier and more robust – and allow them to support more wildlife. Canadian forestry researchers estimate that in a new warming their forest growth would increase by 20 percent. In fact, the world's crops, forests, and soils may well be nature's "missing carbon sink." (Not all human-produced carbon dioxide shows up in the atmosphere or is absorbed by the surface layers of the ocean, which suggests that it is being used by plants.)

Of course, it would put less stress on our wild species if the world always stayed at the same temperature, but the planet has never done that. Our "species models" mostly evolved in the Cambrian Period (six-hundred-million years ago), and they have

17

already survived several ice ages and hot spells....

DECREASE IN DISASTERS

Most of the trillion-dollar estimates of global warming "costs" headlined in the 1980s were based on forecasts that locales such as New York City and Bangladesh would be drowned under rising seas. In 1980, for example, some activists claimed that global warming would raise sea levels by twenty-five feet. In 1985, a National Research Council panel estimated a three-foot rise in the sea level. Those are frightening scenarios, but completely untrue.

The Medieval Climate Optimum did not produce devastating floods. Nor will a new global warming. It may seem paradoxical, but a modest warming in the polar regions will actually mean more arctic ice, not less. The polar ice caps depend on snowfall, and polar air is normally very cold and dry. If polar temperatures warm a few degrees, there will be more moisture in the air – and more snowfall, and more polar ice....

The smaller the temperature difference between the North Pole and the equator, the milder the weather. Most of the warming, if it occurs, will be toward the poles, with very little increase near the equator. Thus, there would be less of the temperature difference that drives big storms.

Forging onward intrepidly, some alarmists have claimed that a warmer world would suffer huge increases in deaths from horrible plagues of malaria, yellow fever, and other warm-climate diseases. One study predicted fifty- to eighty-million more cases of malaria alone per year. (There are now approximately five-hundred million new cases of malaria each year, and up to 2.7 million deaths.)

Fortunately, these claims are unlikely to come true, because they ignore some important, fundamental realities. As mentioned, global warming would be very slight near the equator and thus would only slightly expand the range of the malarial mosquitoes. Hence there is little reason to expect tropical plagues to increase naturally.

Moreover, these diseases are nowhere near as relentless as the scare scenarios assume. In the U.S., for example, malaria and yellow fever once ranged from New Orleans to Chicago. We conquered those diseases, however, and not by changing the climate. We did it by suppressing mosquitoes, creating vaccines, and putting screens on doors, windows, and porches. Other countries can do the same. Third World countries have had high disease rates because they were poor, not because warm climates cannot be made safe....

WHY BE WARY?

The original global warming scare stories were authored by eco-activists who have subsequently admitted that they were looking for ways to persuade people to live leaner lifestyles. To frighten us into lowering our living standards, they have announced a whole series of terrifying claims, most of which have already been proven wrong.

- Activists frequently warned us that the human population would reach fifteen billion, or fifty billion, or whatever astronomic level would collapse the ecosystem. We now know that affluence and contraceptives will give the world a peak population of 8.5 billion around the year 2035, followed by a slow decline in the late twenty-first century.

- Activists warned us that acid rain from industrial pollution would destroy forests in the First World. A billion dollars' worth of research has shown that acid rain is a very minor problem due mainly to natural factors.

- We are still looking for the first case of human cancer from pesticide residues, and the National Research Council (NRC) says that we will probably never find one. Moreover, as the NRC reports, "A sound recommendation for cancer prevention

19

is to increase fruit and vegetable intake." Thus pesticides are actually helping cut cancer rates by producing more plentiful, affordable, and attractive fruits and vegetables....

A POVERTY OF ENERGY

"But what if we're right?" the activists respond. History says that they are not. And the problem is, the "solutions" these activists recommend, however well-intended, would leave much of the world without an energy system – and that would be deadly for both people and animals. If we were to triple the cost of coal, double the cost of oil, ban nuclear power, and tear out hydroelectric dams – which would be the result of the activists' approach – humanity would essentially be left without energy.

Solar and wind power are extremely expensive and undependable. Burning large amounts of renewable wood would destroy huge tracts of forest – and the animals that live there. And in a world of expensive energy, people would not be able to afford the window screens, latrines, clean water, and refrigeration that prevent millions of deaths per year. Diarrhea, due mainly to spoiled food and untreated water, is the number one child-killer on the planet. Refrigeration has helped cut stomach cancer rates by three-quarters in the First World.

The widespread poverty caused by expensive energy would reverse the current worldwide trend toward greater affluence, decreasing birth rates, and better health. The low-energy option would destroy millions of square miles of wildlife habitat. High energy taxes would all but destroy modern agriculture, with its tractors and nitrogen fertilizer (produced mainly with natural gas). Shifting back to draft animals would mean clearing millions of additional acres of forest to feed the beasts of burden.

Giving up nitrogen fertilizer would mean clearing five to six million square miles of forest to grow clover and other nitrogen-fixing "green manure" crops. The losses of wilderness would nearly equal the combined land area of the United States and Brazil.

History and the emerging science of climatology tell us that we need not fear a return of the Little Climate Optimum. If there is any global warming in the twenty-first century, it will produce the kind of milder, more pleasant weather that marked the Medieval Little Optimum – with the added benefit of more carbon dioxide in the atmosphere and therefore a more luxuriant natural environment....

GLOBAL WARMING: BUST FOR THE SOUTH

Patrick Nunn

Patrick Nunn is a Professor and Head of Geography at the University of the South Pacific. As leader of its Climate Change Researchers' Group, he has been involved in climate-change issues in the Pacific islands for more than ten years. Nunn is the author of the book Oceanic Islands *(Blackwell, 1994).*

■ POINTS TO CONSIDER

1. According to Nunn, what is the greatest stress, produced by global warming, that affects the Pacific Rim? What is its consequence on human activity?

2. List two factors that make establishing a global warming trend difficult for Pacific islands.

3. What evidence exists showing a global warming trend?

4. Cite two factors that lead to a rise in sea level.

5. What does the author from the previous reading believe to be the effects of global warming on latitudes closer to the equator?

Excerpted from Nunn, Patrick. "Global Warming." **New Internationalist**. June 1997: 20-1. Reprinted by permission, **New Internationalist**, Toronto. Subscription (Canada) $38.50 (includes $2.94 GST) – individual 1 year, $64.20 (includes $4.20 GST) – institution 1 year –35 Riviera Drive, Unit 17, Markham, ON L3R 8N4, (905) 946-0407, (905) 946-0410 (fax), magazine@indas.on.can. Subscription (United States) $35.98 – individual 1 year, $60.00 – institution 1 year, PO Box 1143, Lewiston, NY 14092, (905) 946-0407, (905) 946-0410 (fax).

There seems little reason to doubt that the Pacific has been warming at approximately the same rate as almost everywhere else.

The Pacific most tourists see is the stuff of fantasy. Behind the veneer, however, lie environments under considerable stress. The worst symptoms of this stress have been caused by resource mismanagement and the never-ending search for export dollars. But another problem looms large over Pacific island nations as they struggle to sustain themselves into the twenty-first century – and that is global warming.

NON-INDUSTRIALIZED COUNTRIES

The evidence that our planet's surface has been warming for the past 100 years or so is overwhelming. Yet the data on which this evidence is based comes largely from industrialized countries – not from small Pacific islands with only minuscule industrial sectors. Long-term, regularly monitored climate stations are few in the Pacific and data quality is often suspect. So there has been some doubt about whether global warming has indeed affected this vast region.

Yet the three best sites – in Fiji, Hawaii and Aotearoa/New Zealand – all show an unequivocal result. The Fiji data from Government House in Suva, for example, show a net rise of around 0.5°C from 1884 until 1986, when the recording station was relocated. There seems little reason to doubt that the Pacific has been warming at approximately the same rate as almost everywhere else. Throughout history climate has been changing. So too has the surface of the oceans. The connection is twofold. Just as water expands slightly when heated, so does the upper part of the ocean when its temperature rises. Ice will melt when heated – but, if it is floating, the sea level will not change. This will happen only if the ice is on land. When temperatures rise, through both thermal expansion of ocean water and land-ice melt, the sea level will rise.

The sea level in the Pacific is undoubtedly rising and has been for at least 100 years – probably twice as long. The few long-term tide-gauge records that we have suggest that it has been rising at a rate of around 1.5 millimeters per year. This may not sound very threatening. But on a gently sloping coastline a rise of around 15 centimeters, similar to that of the past 100 years, can cause flooding of tens of meters of shoreline....

Admittedly the hard evidence is not as good as that for temperature. Skeptics have tended to latch onto tide-gauge records. Because they are too short – less than 30 years – and/or because the place where the tide gauge is located is itself moving, they do not show a clear pattern of sea level rise....

DAUNTING PROSPECTS

Projections by the sophisticated computer models of the Intergovernmental Panel on Climate Change (IPCC) – the group of some 700 experts given this task in 1987 by the UN – suggest that the rates of temperature and sea level rise will increase three- to five-fold in the next 100 years or so. The effects of the past century will be dwarfed by those of the next. To understand what this means for the Pacific islands we need to appreciate something of their variety.

The nations of Kiribati, Marshall Islands, Tokelau and Tuvalu are not particularly populous, nor do they have great land areas. Yet all the land they have rises less than about four meters above mean sea level. Not only are their islands low but they are built largely from loose sand and gravel chucked up during large storms onto the reefs which surround them.

Traditionally the people of these islands have been dependent on what they can catch to eat from nearby reefs. Parts of Tarawa atoll in Kiribati, for example, now have a population density similar to that of Hong Kong. In some places reefs are becoming overexploited. Root crops are also grown in pits sunk into the shallow freshwater lens beneath the island surface. Sea level rise is causing erosion of these islands and also – because the surface of the lens is controlled by that of the sea surface – increased freshwater flooding.

NOT OUR PROBLEM

Most other Pacific nations comprise largely high islands. This is another reason for the common perception of their governments that sea level rise is "not our problem." Yet 29 per cent or more of the people live along their coasts. Their traditional use of coastal resources is much the same as in the low islands. Many of the coastal plains have equivalent problems of erosion and freshwater flooding. The latter effect is exacerbated by rivers bursting out of their channels at the same time as high tides are raising water-table levels.

Economic activity is mostly located along the coasts. Take commercial agriculture in Fiji, for example. Sugar cane – the third-biggest foreign-currency earner – is grown mostly on flat areas along coasts or on low-lying river deltas. Over the last 50 years or so increasing seawater penetration of coastal aquifers has been identified as a reason for falling sugar content in cane. Research is currently being pursued to develop more salt-tolerant strains of sugar cane and other crops.

BEACH EROSION

Or take tourism – increasingly important as a source of revenue throughout the Pacific islands. Tourists are attracted by sun, sand and sea. But tourist beaches are being eroded by sea level rise. Some resort owners spend huge amounts of money maintaining a beach which 50 years ago maintained itself. Ambitious schemes for tourist resorts built on reclaimed land throughout the Pacific islands seek investors' dollars, oblivious, it seems, of the estimates of the IPCC.

The coral reefs which surround most tropical Pacific island groups are not only important sources of sustenance for islanders, but also provide physical protection to many island shores. Huge waves whipped up by storms or driven across the ocean by undersea earthquakes would cause massive damage to island coasts were it not for the buffering effects of offshore reefs....

FUTURE STRESS

Many coral reefs are under stress for human-associated reasons. If ocean temperatures and sea levels rise as predicted then this stress will increase, perhaps to such a degree that entire reefs might die or be unable to act as such effective buffers. The cause of future stress is not simply that sea level rise will drown reef surfaces, denying sunlight to photosynthetic reef organisms. Rising temperatures will combine with other sources of stress to cause widespread coral death by "bleaching." When the water surrounding a coral is heated beyond about 32°C that coral is prone to eject the symbiotic algae which live within it and give reefs such glorious colors. In this way they become "bleached" and die. Incidents of coral bleaching have already been recorded in French

Polynesia and on Aitutaki in the Cook Islands.

Optimistic but unrealistic observers have been quick to assure Pacific island governments that, if sea level does rise as fast as the IPCC contends, then "don't worry," all the reefs will grow upwards just as fast. This will not happen. For although some Pacific reefs have done so in the past, this was not a Pacific-wide phenomenon and happened long before people entered the picture and created such high levels of stress in these fragile ecosystems.

"WAIT-AND-SEE"

Fate has conspired to create an impression among many Pacific island governments that global warming poses less serious problems to their nations than is likely, given the present state of knowledge. Many island governments have adopted a "wait-and-see" policy. They argue that, before they commit resources which are earmarked for other, potentially more pressing, problems they should have some concrete evidence.

There are other reasons behind this attitude. Many government decision-makers see global warming as a problem which was not created in the Pacific islands but in the metropolitan countries of northwest Europe and the Pacific Rim. These countries should bear the financial brunt of their profligacy in the Pacific islands....

GLOBAL WARMING: BOON FOR THE NORTH

Thomas Gale Moore

Thomas Gale Moore is a Senior Fellow at the Hoover Institute at Stanford University. He served as a member of the President's Council of Economic Advisors between 1985-89. An author of numerous books and scholarly articles, Moore has also taught at numerous academic institutions including Michigan State University, the Carnegie Institute of Technology, the Stanford University Graduate School of Business, and UCLA.

■ POINTS TO CONSIDER

1. According to the Intergovernmental Panel of Climate Change (IPCC), will global warming be measurable in the next century? If so, by how much?

2. In the industrialized North, is the mortality rate more affected by hot or cold, according to the author? How will global warming affect human health in colder latitudes?

3. Discuss global warming's effect on the economies of colder latitudes.

4. According to the reading, what effect will global warming have upon warmer latitudes – closer to the equator? What should the industrialized North's policy be toward the global South with regard to global warming?

Excerpted from Moore, Thomas Gale. **Climate of Fear: Why We Shouldn't Worry about Global Warming.** Washington, D.C.: Cato Institute, 1998. Reprinted with permission.

...Our modern industrial economy is less affected by weather than are societies heavily dependent on nature. Higher average temperatures can bring many benefits, including longer growing seasons, a healthier and longer-lived population, and reduced transportation and communication costs.

...A media chorus, led by such prestigious organizations as the *New York Times,* the Public Broadcasting System, and *Scientific American,* has fanned the fear of climate change. Reputable scientists, including Bert Bolin (Stockholm University), Benjamin Santer (Lawrence Livermore National Laboratory), Robert Watson (Office of Science and Technology Policy, White House), and Stephen Schneider (Stanford University) have claimed that the climate is changing or will shift, and that measures are urgently needed to head off potential disaster. If these prophets are accurate, we must move quickly to slash the emission of greenhouse gases. Before we leap, however, we should be clear that such policies, which may be unnecessary, would be inordinately expensive and would lead to worldwide recession, rising unemployment, civil disturbances, and increased tension between nations as accusations of cheating and violations of international treaties inflamed passions....

UNCERTAIN OUTCOME

Climatologists do not agree on the effect of greenhouse gases on climate. For an effective doubling of CO_2, the United Nations' Intergovernmental Panel on Climate Change (IPCC) and many other experts predict a likely increase in average temperatures from $2.5°$ to $6.5°$ Fahrenheit, with the most likely boost being $4.5°$. Other climatologists, such as Richard Lindzen (MIT), S. Fred Singer (Science and Environmental Policy Project), and Patrick Michaels (University of Virginia), predict negligible or only small warming. Nevertheless, most researchers do believe that, if man continues to seed the atmosphere with CO_2, climate change will occur, if it has not already started. Change is normally feared, thus many are apprehensive at the prospect. It is also true that people believe what it is in their interest to believe. If global climate change is viewed as a threat, environmental organizations can raise more support from the public; politicians can posture as protectors of mankind; newspapers can write more scary stories, thus increasing circulation; and scientists, even those most skeptical, can justify research grants to study the issue.

THE BENEFITS OF GLOBAL WARMING

Economic forecasts of the influence of climate change on human activity also vary considerably. Some predict that people will benefit from any such change while others view the possibility with great alarm....

History and research support the proposition that a warmer climate is beneficial. Past warm periods have seen dramatic improvements in civilization and human well-being. Fortunately, our modern industrial economy is less affected by weather than are societies heavily dependent on nature. Higher average temperatures can bring many benefits, including longer growing seasons, a healthier and longer-lived population, and reduced transportation and communication costs. Although not everyone will find a warmer climate in his or her better interest, the evidence shows that most individuals, especially those living in higher latitudes, will experience a gain. Climate change will probably be small in tropical areas, so the population of equatorial regions will be largely unaffected....

REDUCTIONS IN DISEASE

Most of the causes of premature death have nothing to do with climate. Worldwide the leading cause is chronic disease – accounting for 24 million deaths in 1996 – such as maladies of the circulatory system, cancers, mental disorders, chronic respiratory conditions, and musculoskeletal disorders, none of which has anything to do with climate but everything to do with aging (*World Health Report* 1997, vol. 2, no. 1.). Another 17 million, most of them in poor countries, succumbed in the same year to disorders caused by infections or parasites, such as diarrhea, tuberculosis, measles, and malaria. Many of those diseases are unrelated to climate; most have to do with poverty....

The increase in average temperatures during this century has apparently been accompanied by a decline in hot weather deaths relative to winter mortality. Before the early or middle part of the century, deaths during the summer months were much higher relative to winter than is currently the case (Momiyama 1977). Perhaps the decline in physical labor, which is afflicted with a much higher rate of fatal accidents than office work, helps to explain the change. One Japanese scholar, Masako Momiyama, however, reports that for most advanced countries, such as the

United States, Japan, United Kingdom, France, and Germany, mortality is now concentrated in the winter....

Although it is impossible to measure the gains exactly, a moderately warmer climate would be likely to benefit Americans in many ways, especially in health. At the same time, let me stress that the evidence presented here is for a moderate rise in temperatures. If warming were to continue well beyond 4.5°F, the costs would mount and at some point the health effects would undoubtedly turn negative. Contrary to many dire forecasts, however, the temperature increase predicted by the IPCC, which is now less than 4.5°F, under a doubling of greenhouse gases would yield health benefits for Americans....

A warmer climate should improve health and extend life, at least for Americans and probably for Europeans, the Japanese, and people living in high latitudes. High death rates in the tropics appear to be more a function of poverty than of climate....

ECONOMIC GAINS

Casual analysis of the economic effects of climate change demonstrates that most modern industries are relatively immune to weather. Climate affects principally agriculture, forestry, and fishing, which together constitute less than two percent of U.S. gross domestic product (GDP). Manufacturing, most service industries, and nearly all extractive industries remain unaffected by climate shifts. Factories can be built in northern Sweden or Canada or in Texas, Central America, or Mexico. Higher temperatures will leave mining largely untouched; oil drilling in the northern seas and mining in the mountains might even benefit. Banking, insurance, medical services, retailing, education, and a variety of other services can prosper as well in warm climates (with air conditioning) as in cold (with central heating). A warmer climate will lower transportation costs: less snow and ice to torment truckers and automobile drivers; fewer winter storms to disrupt air travel – bad weather in the summer has fewer disruptive effects and passes quickly; a lower incidence of storms and less fog will make shipping less risky. Fuel consumption for heating will decline, while that for air conditioning will increase.

Inhabitants of the advanced industrial countries would scarcely notice a rise in worldwide temperatures. As modern societies have developed a larger industrial base and become more service-oriented, they have grown less dependent on farming, thus boosting their immunity to variations in weather....

In many parts of the world, warmer weather should mean longer growing seasons. Should the world warm, the hotter climate would enhance evaporation from the seas, leading most probably to more precipitation worldwide. Moreover, the enrichment of the atmosphere with CO_2 would fertilize plants and make for more vigorous growth. Agricultural economists studying the relationship of temperatures and CO_2 to crop yields have found not only that a warmer climate would push up yields in Canada, Australia, Japan, northern Russia, Finland, and Iceland but also that the added boost from enriched CO_2 fertilization would enhance output by 17 percent (Wittwer 1995, 1997).

Several scientists have recently reported that the increased concentration of CO_2 has produced an increase from 1981 to 1991 in plant growth in the northern high latitudes (Myneni et al. 1997). More vigorous plant development, while possibly choking out a few species, provides a more plentiful habitat for animals.

Rising sea levels would, of course, impose costs on low-lying regions, including a number of islands and delta areas. For the United States – assuming a three-foot rise in sea level, at the high end of predictions for the year 2100 – economists have estimated the costs of building dikes and levees and the loss of land at seven billion dollars to $10.6 billion annually, or less than 0.2 percent of GDP (Cline 1992, 109). For some small island nations, of course, the problems could be much more severe and their hardships should be addressed....

FOREIGN AID ISSUE

Some may be willing to grant that rich industrial countries in temperate climates might benefit, yet argue that the poor Third World areas will suffer. The IPCC Working Group III report asserts: "...climate change seems likely to impose greater risks and damage on poorer regions " (IPCC 1995c, 84). Chapter Three of that report on "Equity and Social Considerations" argues strongly that poor countries are much more vulnerable, hence rich nations should bear the burden. Not only has the West produced most of the greenhouse gases to date – the rapidly growing Third World will soon exceed the output of industrialized countries – but the rich nations can afford to pay the cost of slowing or stop-

30

ping global climate change and to contribute to any measures necessary to adapt to change. Climate policy has become foreign aid.

Poor countries dependent on agriculture are more sensitive to changes in climate. But the growth of CO_2 should actually help. Many of these nations are in tropical areas and will be largely unaffected because the climate will not change appreciably near the equator. Other subtropical regions should receive more rainfall and may benefit, although farmers may need to learn to grow new crops. Some low-lying countries – Bangladesh, for example – may suffer from more frequent sea flooding as water levels rise. Such places, including low-lying islands, may be the only major losers from warming. Rather than spend resources on a futile effort to slow warming, it might be more humane to help them either to accelerate their growth so they become less dependent on the weather, or to build dikes for protection from rising seas, as the Netherlands has done. Foreign aid should not be confused with environmental policy....

CONCLUSION

For most of the world, the cost of warming over the next 100 years would be either very small or an actual benefit. As noted earlier, most people in most places will be better off in a warmer world. Those poor parts of the world that might suffer the most should have help. In any case, delaying action by 20 to 30 years appears to be the only truly prudent, "no-regrets" policy. Technology will advance. Incomes in Third World countries will multiply. The world will be more capable of coping with change, whatever vicissitudes may occur....

THICK CHECKBOOKS

According to John Shanahan of the Alexis de Tocqueville Institute, environmental PACs spent over a half million dollars in the 1995-1996 election cycle.

These supposedly nonpolitical groups were, in fact, quite partisan. Nineteen out of every $20 went to Democrats. An incredible 96 percent of the candidates targeted for defeat were Republicans....

Doug Bandow. "Environmental Lobby Is a Paper Tiger." **Conservative Chronicle.** Jan . 15, 1997: 21. ©1997 Copley News Service.

Cline, William, 1992. **The Economics of Global Warming.** Washington: Institute for International Economics.

Intergovernmental Panel on Climate Change, 1995c. **Summary for Policy Makers: The Economic and Social Dimensions of Climate Change.** Prepared by Working Group III.

Momiyama, Masako, 1977. **Seasonality in Human Mortality.** Tokyo: University of Tokyo.

Myneni, R.B., et al., 1997. "Increased Plant Growth in the Northern High Latitudes from 1981 to 1991." **Nature** 386 (April 17).

Wittwer, S.H. 1995. "Food, Climate and Carbon Dioxide." Boca Raton, Fla.: CRC Press, 1997. "The Global Environment: It's Good for Food Production." In **State of the Climate Report.** Edited by P.J. Michaels. Arlington, Va.: New Hope Environmental Services, Western Funds Association.

World Health Organization, 1997. **World Health Report.** Geneva, Switzerland.

READING

5

THE SCIENCE OF GLOBAL WARMING: THE POINT

E. Calvin Beisner

E. Calvin Beisner, Associate Professor of Interdisciplinary Studies at Covenant College of Lookout Mountain, Georgia, is a correspondent for World. World *is a weekly magazine of politics and culture which describes its mission as follows: "to help Christians apply the Bible to their understanding of and response to everyday current events."*

■ POINTS TO CONSIDER

1. Why does Beisner discount Al Gore's claim of a scientific consensus on global warming?

2. How does the reading try to prove a scientific consensus "that flatly denies the crisis scenario" for global warming?

3. According to the article, what global temperature trends have been observed?

4. Assess the consequence of the global temperature trends reported in the article to global warming theory.

Excerpted from Beisner, E. Calvin. "Putting Kyoto on Ice." **World.** Aug. 8, 1998: 12-6. Reprinted with permission.

...the best scientific evidence does not indicate that global average temperatures have risen in recent decades.

...The appearance of consensus was strong enough that Vice President Al Gore could announce at a White House conference on global warming, "The overwhelming balance of evidence and scientific opinion is that it is no longer a theory but now a fact that global warming is real." In support of this claim, Mr. Gore touted "2,500 scientists" who endorsed the UN's 1996 Intergovernmental Panel on Climate Change (IPCC) report with its forecast of catastrophic global warming.

COMPLEX TREND

Even when Mr. Gore made the claim that "2,500 scientists" had endorsed the IPCC report, it was false. As atmospheric physicist S. Fred Singer, president of the Science and Environmental Policy Project, pointed out at the time, "If one were to add up all contributors and reviewers listed in the three IPCC reports published in 1996, one would count about 2,100. The great majority of these are not conversant with the intricacies of atmospheric physics, although some may know a lot about forestry, fisheries, or agriculture. Most are social scientists – or just policy experts and government functionaries...The list even includes known skeptics of global warming – much to their personal and professional chagrin."

Mr. Singer pointed out that "the IPCC report has some 80 authors for its 11 chapters, but only a handful actually wrote the Policymakers' Summary; most of the several hundred listed 'contributors' are simply specialists who allowed their work to be cited, without necessarily endorsing the other chapters or the summary."

By contrast, nearly 100 climate scientists signed the "Leipzig Declaration on Global Climate Change" in 1996, stating, in part, "there does not exist today a general scientific consensus about the importance of greenhouse warming from rising levels of carbon dioxide. In fact, many climate specialists now agree that actual observations from weather satellites show no global warming whatsoever – in direct contradiction to computer model results."

Four years earlier, two other groups had spoken out against the Global Climate Treaty and the conventional wisdom that supports it: More than a hundred U.S. climate scientists signed a "Statement by Atmospheric Scientists on Greenhouse Warming," and eventually more than 4,000 scientists worldwide signed the "Heidelberg Appeal," circulated at the Earth Summit in Rio de Janeiro. But those efforts to get a word in edgewise fell largely on deaf ears....

NO CRISIS AT HAND

In 1998, Arthur B. Robinson, director of the Oregon Institute of Science and Medicine, in cooperation with Frederick Seitz, one of America's premier scientists and past president of the National Academy of Sciences and of Rockefeller University, began circulating a "Global Warming Petition" that flatly denies the crisis scenario and firmly opposes the Kyoto Climate Accord.

Accompanying the petition was an extensive, heavily documented paper reviewing the main scientific literature on greenhouse theory. "The empirical evidence of actual measurements of Earth's temperature shows no man-made warming trend," the paper reported. "Indeed, over the past two decades, when CO_2 levels have been at their highest, global average temperatures have actually cooled slightly."

Initially, the petition went by mail to a variety of scientists. Those who signed and returned cards could ask for more cards to give to colleagues. Then it was put on the Internet so that scientists who wanted to add their signatures could download the petition and signature card, print it out, sign it, and return it. The response has been overwhelming.

By mid-April 1998, more than 15,000 American scientists had signed. By mid-July, the total number of signers had grown to over 18,800. Of these, 16,400 are basic and applied scientists, and nearly all of them have technical training suitable for evaluation of the relevant research data. These include 2,300 physicists, geophysicists, climatologists, meteorologists, oceanographers, and environmental scientists specially qualified to evaluate the effects of carbon dioxide on Earth's atmosphere and climate, and 4,700 chemists, biochemists, biologists, and other life scientists specially qualified to evaluate the effects of carbon dioxide on Earth's plant and animal life.

Defenders of the conventional wisdom initially questioned the credibility of the list. But of the 18,800 signatures so far in the database, 17,300 – including over 95 percent of those holding Ph.D. degrees – have been independently verified, and the other 1,500 are pending verification....

SCIENCE

The best scientific evidence does not indicate that global average temperatures have risen in recent decades. According to greenhouse theory, as carbon dioxide and other greenhouse gas concentrations in the atmosphere rise, thus keeping more solar energy from reflecting from the surface of the globe back into space, average global temperatures should rise.

Yet while there is reasonably good evidence that global average temperatures rose by about 0.6 degrees Centigrade from 1880 to 1980, the data are inconsistent with the theory both because the theory would have predicted nearly three times the increase in temperature for the period and because about 70 percent of the temperature increase that did occur came before 1940 while about 80 percent of the greenhouse gas increase came after 1940. Thus, temperature increase preceded greenhouse gas increase, which is the opposite of what the theory predicts.

The most thorough and reliable data indicate a slight cooling trend from at least 1979 to the present. In the past, most temperature data came from thousands of monitoring stations, mostly on land, mostly in the Northern Hemisphere, and mostly near urban areas. Consequently, they were highly unrepresentative of the globe as a whole and subject to what climatologists have come to call the "urban heat island" effect – the tendency for urban areas to generate and trap their own heat, thus raising local temperatures slightly while having no measurable effect on global temperature. Climatologists have understood the problems with such data for years and have tried to compensate for them, but their means of compensation always required some assumptions about climate as a whole that could not be sustained by data alone.

COOLING TREND

Since 1979, however, they have had access to another source of temperature data that is completely unaffected by urban heat island phenomena. That was the year NASA's Satellite Microwave Sounding Unit, or MSU, went into operation. It measures temper-

"Keep your speeches short. The world's climate is already warm enough without a lot of unnecessary hot air."

Cartoon by Bruce Beattie. Reprinted with permission, **Copley News Service.**

atures in the lower troposphere (the part of the atmosphere nearest the surface of the earth) literally all over the globe.

The data from the MSU, reported by atmospheric scientist James Angell of the Oak Ridge National Laboratory in *Trends Online: A Compendium of Data on Global Change,* and analyzed by leading climatologists R.W. Spencer and J.R. Christy in articles in *Science* in 1990 and *Nature* in 1997, show a decline in global average temperature from 1979 through 1997 that averages about 0.047 degrees Centigrade per decade – or a total decline of about 0.09 degrees over the 19-year period.

Two critics of the MSU's data, Frank J. Wentz and Matthias Schabel, pointed out that the satellite had lost about 15 kilometers in altitude (from an initial 850 kilometers) due to atmospheric drag. The loss in altitude would have resulted in a fictitious decline in temperature readings.

Mr. Spencer acknowledges that the glitch appears genuine. However, he argues that orbital procession in the satellite and calibration drift in the radiometer would have created a false warming trend, offsetting the false cooling trend. This appears confirmed by the fact that there is strong correlation between the MSU temperature data and independently gathered balloon radiosonde temperature data. If the satellite data were really falsified by the decline in altitude, the correlation should disappear. It doesn't.

For the present, at any rate, the combined MSU and balloon radiosonde data appear to be the best available for measuring global average temperature, and the roughly 0.05 degrees Centigrade per decade decline in temperature since 1979 seems real.

GAS UP, TEMPERATURE DOWN

That presents a major problem for global warming theory, because it means temperatures have declined during the very period when carbon dioxide and other atmospheric greenhouse gas concentrations have risen most rapidly – precisely the opposite of what the theory predicts.

But what accounts for the warming widely acknowledged to have taken place from the mid-19th century to the mid-20th? It appears that this was part of a much longer-term recovery from the "Little Ice Age" – a recovery that began about three centuries ago. The "Little Ice Age" itself had followed what climate historians call the "Medieval Climate Optimum," when temperatures well above today's permitted the colonization of Greenland. But with the onset of the "Little Ice Age," the Greenland colonies proved uninhabitable.

The most likely cause of such long-term variations in Earth's temperature is variation in solar energy output. Long-term solar energy output cycles correlate well with long-term geological temperature cycles....

READING

6

THE PUBLIC RELATIONS OF GLOBAL WARMING: THE COUNTERPOINT

Sheldon Rampton and Bob Burton

Sheldon Rampton is Associate Editor of PR Watch *and co-author, with John Stauber, of* Toxic Sludge Is Good for You *(Common Courage Press: 1995). Bob Burton is a reporter based in Australia.* PR Watch *is a publication of the Center for Media and Democracy in Madison, Wisconsin. Contact the Center at 3318 Gregory St., Madison, WI 53711, phone (608) 233-3346, fax (608) 238-2236, www.prwatch.org. Part of the information for this story was provided by Clearinghouse on Environmental Advocacy and Research (CLEAR); by Ross Gelbspan, author of* The Heat Is On; *and by Sharon Beder, author of* Global Spin: The Corporate Assault on Environmentalism.

■ POINTS TO CONSIDER

1. Describe at least three privately funded climate-study organizations and their purpose, according to the article.

2. Explain Australia's role in the global warming debate.

3. What do the authors mean by "front-group?" Why were more of these created in the wake of the Kyoto Conference on Global Climate Change?

4. Examine U.S. policy, as described by the reading, over the past years. What does the article suggest is the consequence of U.S. policy?

Adapted from Burton, Bob and Sheldon Rampton. "The PR Plot to Overheat the Earth." **Earth Island Journal.** Spring 1998: 29-36. Reprinted with permission.

*In 1991, a U.S. corporate coalition created a public
relations front called the Information Council for the
Environment. ICE launched a $500,000 advertising
and PR blitz to "reposition global warming as theory
(not fact)."*

In 1995, the International Panel on Climate Change (IPCC) – a working group of 2,500 climate experts sponsored by the United Nations – bluntly warned that the burning of oil, coal and gasoline has pushed the Earth into a period of climactic instability likely to cause "widespread economic, social and environmental dislocation over the next century."

To avert a catastrophe, IPCC called for policy measures to reduce emissions of greenhouse gases to 20 percent below 1990 levels. Such changes, of course, would seriously alter the lucrative *status quo* enjoyed by fuel companies, automobile makers and other large-scale polluters.

POURING ICE ON THE DEBATE

In 1991, a U.S. corporate coalition including the National Coal Association, the Western Fuels Association and Edison Electrical Institute created a public relations front called the Information Council for the Environment. ICE launched a $500,000 advertising and PR blitz to "reposition global warming as theory (not fact)."

ICE used the services of Bracy Williams & Co., a Washington-based PR firm, along with an opinion pollster which identified "older, less-educated males from larger households who are not typically active information-seekers" and "younger, lower-income women" as "good targets for radio advertisements" that would "directly attack the proponents of global warming."

To boost its credibility, ICE created a scientific advisory panel that featured Patrick Michaels from the Department of Environmental Services at the University of Virginia. Michaels has been the leading scientific naysayer on global warming.

JUST ANOTHER VOICE

The industry's propaganda campaign also created a bevy of other front groups. The group currently leading the charge is the

Global Climate Coalition (GCC), a creation of the Burson-Marsteller PR firm.

From its founding in 1989 until the summer of 1997, GCC operated out of the offices of the National Association of Manufacturers. Its members include Amoco, the American Forest & Paper Association, American Petroleum Institute, Shell Oil, Texaco, Chevron, Chrysler, the U.S. Chamber of Commerce, Exxon, General Motors, Ford and more than 40 other corporations and trade associations.

GCC is also represented by the E. Bruce Harrison Company, a subsidiary of PR giant Ruder Finn. In the 1960s it was the Harrison firm that helped lead the pesticide industry's attack on Rachel Carson and her environmental classic, *Silent Spring.*

Since 1994, GCC has spent more than one million dollars a year to downplay the threat of climate change. The National Coal Association spent more than $700,000 on the global climate issue in 1992 and 1993. In 1993, the American Petroleum Institute paid Burson-Marsteller $1.8 million for a computer-driven "grassroots" letter and phone-in campaign that blocked a proposed tax on fossil fuels.

"For perspective, this is only slightly less than the combined yearly expenditures on global warming of the five major environmental groups that focus on climate issues – about $2.1 million, according to officials of the Environmental Defense Fund, the Natural Resources Defense Council, the Sierra Club, the Union of Concerned Scientists, and the World Wildlife Fund," observes journalist Ross Gelbspan, author of *The Heat Is On,* the best book written to date about the issue.

THE AUSTRALIAN CONNECTION

The GCC recognized early on that Australia would play a key role in its campaign. Most major U.S. PR firms – Edelman's, Burson-Marsteller, Hill & Knowlton, Ketchum, Shandwick and others – have established a presence Down Under.

Australia accounts for more than 30 percent of world trade in coal and has major metal smelting industries that belch greenhouse gases. As a result, Australia has the highest per capita emission of greenhouse gases, equal to that of Asia, even though its population is only one percent of Asia's 2.5 billion people.

41

In 1988, Australia had one of the "greenest" governments in the world. Since then, however, corporations and their front groups have systematically manipulated public opinion through frequent media pronouncements by industry-funded scientists.

These efforts, combined with intensive mining industry lobbying aimed at Australian Prime Minister John Howard, have successfully transformed the Australian government from a green role-model to a green pariah. Rather than agreeing to a call for reductions in greenhouse gas emissions, Australia has announced plans to increase its emissions 18 percent by the year 2010.

Part of the campaign has been managed by Noel Bushnell of Hannagan and Bushnell, which serves as a PR consultant to the Australian Industry Greenhouse Network. Hannagan was formerly the public affairs manager for the Aluminum Corporation of America (Alcoa). Alcoa is 40 percent owned by the Western Mining Corporation, which also owns chemical plants and smelters in Australia, Guinea, Suriname, Jamaica, Brazil, Germany, India, Holland, Japan and the U.S.

COUNTDOWN TO KYOTO

One of the key people building the trans-Pacific campaign was R.J. Smith, Senior Environmental Scholar with the Competitive Enterprise Institute (CEI) – an industry-funded right-wing think-tank based in Washington, D.C.

In a strategy meeting held in November 1996 at CEI headquarters, Ray Evans from Australia's Western Mining Corporation, along with a senior world vice-president for Ford Motors, American Petroleum Institute executive director Bill O'Keefe and Dick Lawson, the executive director of the U.S. National Mining Association, decided to plan "a series of conferences before Kyoto."

The first event – held on July 15, 1997 in Washington, D.C. – was called "The Costs of Kyoto." It predicted staggering economic costs for any policies aimed at restricting emissions.

Speakers included Fran Smith from Consumer Alert, an industry-funded front group; Patrick Michaels of ICE; Australian Embassy Chief of Mission Paul O'Sullivan and Brian Fisher from the Australian Bureau of Agriculture and Resource Economics (ABARE), a government-funded economic forecasting agency that has predicted huge costs in jobs and income if emission reduction targets are met.

For a contribution of $50,000 corporations can buy a seat on ABARE's steering committee. "By becoming a member of the consortium, you will have an influence on the direction of the model development," ABARE states in promotional material to potential sponsors. Contributors to ABARE's work include Rio Tinto, the world's largest mining company; Texaco; Mobil Oil; Exxon; the Australian Coal Association; the Australian Aluminum Council; and Statoil, the Norwegian oil company. All told, ABARE receives $500,000 a year from the fossil fuel industry.

Rather than setting a goal for all nations to lower their greenhouse emissions by equal proportions, ABARE advocated "differentiated" goals tailored to the economic characteristics of each country. According to environmentalists, differentiation would scuttle any hope of effectively capping worldwide emissions.

At an August 1997 CEI-sponsored conference in Canberra, former U.S. Senator Malcolm Wallop declared: "This conference is the first shot across the bow of those who expect to champion the Kyoto Treaty."

Wallop chairs the Frontiers of Freedom Institute, another corporate-funded U.S. think-tank. Joining Wallop at the conference were U.S. Senator Chuck Hagel (R-NE), U.S. Congressman John Dingell (D-MI), and Richard Lawson, president of the U.S. National Mining Association.

WHO'S BEHIND THE FRONT-GROUPS?

In the U.S., the countdown to Kyoto saw a dizzying array of activity from industry front-groups:

The Global Climate Information Project (GCIP), launched by some of the nation's most powerful trade associations, spent more than three million dollars in newspaper and television advertising.

The GCIP's ads were produced by Goddard* Claussen/First Tuesday, a California-based PR firm whose clients include the Chlorine Chemistry Council, the Chemical Manufacturers Association, Dupont Merck Pharmaceuticals and the Vinyl Siding Institute.

The GCIP is represented by Richard Pollock, former director of the Naderite group Critical Mass, who now works as a senior vice president for Shandwick Public Affairs, the second largest PR firm in the U.S. Shandwick's clients include Browning-Ferris Industries, Central Maine Power, Georgia-Pacific, Monsanto, New York State Electric and Gas Co., Ciba-Geigy, Ford, Hydro-Quebec, Pfizer and Proctor & Gamble.

The Coalition for Vehicle Choice (CVC), a front for automobile manufacturers, launched its own advertising campaign, including a three-page ad in the *Washington Post* blasting the climate agreements as an assault on the U.S. economy. Sponsors of the ad included hundreds of oil and gas companies, auto dealers and parts stores, as well as a number of far-right anti-environmental organizations such as the American Land Rights Association and Sovereignty International (which claims that international environmental treaties are part of a UN conspiracy to establish a "new world order" that will abolish private property and personal freedoms).

CVC was originally founded in 1991 to fight higher fuel economy standards. Its 1993 budget was $2.2 million, all of which came from Ford, GM and Chrysler.

The National Center for Public Policy Research, another industry-funded think-tank established the Kyoto Earth Summit Information Center, issued an "Earth Summit Fact Sheet" and fed anti-treaty quotes to the media.

On the eve of the Kyoto Conference, Steven Milloy, executive director of The Advancement of Sound Science Coalition (TASSC), announced that more than 500 physicians and scientists had signed an open letter to world leaders opposing any climate change treaty. When asked to provide the signers' names and credentials, Milloy told the authors that he had not yet had time to "compile" the hard-copy list.

TASSC's funders include 3M, Amoco, Chevron, Dow Chemical, Exxon, General Motors, Lawrence Livermore National Laboratory, Lorillard Tobacco, Louisiana Chemical Association, National Pest Control Association, Occidental Petroleum, Philip Morris, Procter & Gamble, Santa Fe Pacific Gold and W.R. Grace.

The American Policy Center (APC), another far-right, industry-funded nonprofit organization based in Washington, D.C., worked to mobilize a "Strike for Liberty," calling on truckers to pull over to the side of the road for an hour and for farmers to drive tractors into key cities to "shut down the nation" as a protest against any Kyoto treaty.

APC also issued the claim that "Al Gore has said abortion should be used to reduce global warming" and charged that the global warming issue is another Clinton attempt to replace private property with "socialism," "bureaucracy" and "big government."

THE BOTTOM LINE

On the eve of Earth Day 1993, President Clinton announced his intention to sign a treaty on global warming. Ever since then, he has played the game of perpetually watering down the content of any such treaty.

Clinton's October 1993 "Climate Change Action Plan" turned out to be a "voluntary effort" depending entirely on the goodwill of industry for implementation.

By early 1996, he was forced to admit that the plan would not even come close to meeting its goal for greenhouse gas reductions by the year 2000.

In June 1997, Clinton addressed the UN's Rio+5 Earth Summit. Painting a near-apocalyptic picture of encroaching seas and killer heat, he acknowledged that America's record over the past five years was "not sufficient...We must do better and we will."

In October 1997, however, Clinton announced that realistic targets and timetables for cutting greenhouse gas emissions should be put off for 20 years, prompting the London Guardian to editorialize that "champagne corks are popping in the boardrooms of BP, Shell, Esso, Mobil, Ford, General Motors, and the coal, steel and aluminum corporations of the U.S., Australia and Europe...

"In a stunning example of raw backroom power and political manipulation, the 'death-row' industries showed who rules the economic world by effectively killing any hope of combating global warming at the Kyoto climate conference. The new limits are so weak...that two years of hard work by 150 countries towards reaching an agreement are now irrelevant."

The treaty that emerged from Kyoto proposed a reduction of only seven percent in global greenhouse emissions by the year

2012, far below the 30 percent reduction demanded by low-lying island nations that fear massive flooding as melting polar ice leads to rising sea levels.

As the *New York Times* somberly noted on December 12, 1997, even in the unlikely event that the treaty were adopted and strictly observed by all the participating nations, "many experts believe that it may already be too late to avoid serious climactic disruption."

CURBING CO$_2$ EMISSIONS WILL HARM THE ECONOMY

H. Sterling Burnett

H. Sterling Burnett is an environmental policy analyst at the National Center for Policy Analysis (NCPA). He specializes in environmental ethics and policy issues. He is also an advisor to the American Legislative Exchange Council's Energy, Environment, Natural Resources and Agriculture Task Force and Brand Visiting Chair of Free Enterprise and Public Policy at Howard Payne University. NCPA is a nonprofit, public policy research institute in Dallas.

■ POINTS TO CONSIDER

1. Discuss the equity issues Burnett raises with regard to limits on carbon dioxide emissions.

2. What do the facts the author cites indicate about a global warming trend?

3. Describe the implications for the economy, according to the author, of binding limits on CO$_2$ emissions.

4. According to the reading, explain the effect of CO$_2$ limits on the environment.

Burnett, H. Sterling. "Dubious Global Warming Treaty Harms U.S. Workers and Industry." **Human Events.** Jan. 10, 1997: 21. Reprinted with permission, National Center for Policy Analysis.

***...the proposed treaty would place U.S. industries at a
gross competitive disadvantage and for little or no
benefit to the environment.***

In 1992 at the United Nations-sponsored Earth Summit in Rio,
the United States signed a treaty that established voluntary goals
for returning to 1990 levels of greenhouse gas emissions by the
year 2000. Since voluntary action is not working, the Clinton
Administration now wants a new international treaty with enforceable goals.

BINDING LIMITS

At a recent UN conference on climate change in Geneva,
Timothy Wirth, U.S. Undersecretary of State for Global Affairs,
said the Clinton Administration is committed to legally binding
limits on greenhouse gas emissions. This is consistent with the
views Wirth expressed in 1990 when he was a U.S. senator. Wirth
said then: "We've got to ride the global warming issue. Even if the
theory of global warming is wrong, we will be doing the right
thing – in terms of economic policy and environmental policy."

However, because the proposed treaty would be binding only
on developed countries, it would encourage a redistribution of
emissions (and economic growth) from rich to poor countries. As
a result, the treaty would actually harm American industries and
workers, significantly increase the cost of living and contribute
little to reducing global warming – if, in fact, it is occurring.

OPPRESSIVE MEASURES

Ground-level measurements of temperature indicate that the
earth has warmed between 0.3 and 0.6 degrees Celsius in the last
century. In addition, atmospheric carbon dioxide (CO_2), a primary
greenhouse gas, has increased by approximately 25% in the last
century and a half.

From these facts and computer simulations of the climate, some
scientists infer that the earth's current warming is due to the
increase of CO_2 in the atmosphere, caused primarily by the use of
fossil fuels (oil, coal and gas). According to their models, without
a sharp and immediate reduction in the level of CO_2 emissions,
the earth will warm further, causing all manner of calamities. For
instance, some scientists claim that continued global warming

could melt the polar ice caps, raise sea levels and flood coastal cities and low-lying island nations around the globe. Others argue that global warming could cause droughts and floods in increased numbers and of greater severity.

If current trends continue, some scientists estimate a temperature increase of between 0.8 and 3.5 degrees Celsius over the next 100 years. Even if this estimate is correct, it is well within the natural range of known temperature variation over the last 15,000 years.

INSIGNIFICANT WARMING

However, there is little evidence that increased CO_2 has had more than a small part to play in this century's temperature increase. Most of the warming occurred before the 1940s, before the widespread use of automobiles – which produce the vast majority of human-caused CO_2 emissions. And satellite data, the most reliable climate evidence that we have, shows no evidence of warming over the past 14 years.

Based on these facts, some scientists have argued that global warming probably isn't occurring. However, even if it does occur, the change in temperature would be so small as to be negligible; certainly the estimated change would not cause the apocalyptic effects predicted just a few years ago.

Proposals for reducing CO_2 emissions include taxes on fossil fuels and on energy consumption, increased fuel economy standards for cars, subsidized technology sharing, "clean" fuel requirements (such as natural gas) and subsidized production of renewable energy. Alternatively, some have suggested that the U.S. institute a direct rationing scheme, requiring individuals to buy permits to use energy. This would give the government life-or-death power over six-sevenths of the economy, making the administration's infamous health-care plan look tame by comparison.

GRAVE IMPACT

The implications of the proposed climate change commitments for the U.S. economy are grave:

- Some analysts have estimated that meeting the Administration's proposal to cut emissions to ten percent below 1990 levels would reduce U.S. gross domestic product by $200 billion annually.

49

- A DRI/McGraw Hill study projected that over the next 14 years more than 500,000 Americans annually would lose their jobs if the 1992 Rio commitments were implemented.

- The study also estimated that the government would have to increase gas prices by more than 60 cents a gallon and double the price of heating oil just to hold carbon emissions at 1990 levels, and more than double those increases to reduce emissions another ten percent.

A study of the proposed commitments by Constad Research, Inc., estimated that the changes would kill off 1.6 million jobs over the next nine years and put another 3.5 million or so "at risk," primarily in Texas, California, Ohio, Michigan, Pennsylvania and Louisiana.

In addition, the price of food and transportation would rise dramatically. In Geneva, Wirth dismissed these costs by saying, "In a world of change, not everyone can remain advantaged." Yet those most disadvantaged by the policies would be low-income families who spend a higher proportion of their incomes on food and energy.

LITTLE OR NO BENEFIT

Perhaps more disturbing than the rush to legislate based on incomplete and contradictory science is that the proposed treaty would place U.S. industries at a gross competitive disadvantage and for little or no benefit to the environment.

Developing countries would not be bound by the treaty, because in 1995 the U.S. State Department agreed to the Berlin Mandate, which stipulated that new climate change commitments would apply only to developed countries.

Developing countries currently produce more than one-half of all greenhouse gases. According to the International Energy Agency, as much as 85% of the projected increase in CO_2 emissions will come from developing countries – the same countries and regions that are exempted from the proposed treaties (Eastern Europe, Russia, China, India, South Korea, etc.). In fact if developed countries unilaterally stopped all their greenhouse gas emissions immediately (something no one seriously proposes), total greenhouse gas emissions would continue to rise. The UN estimates that exempted countries will contribute 76% of total greenhouse gas emissions within the next 50 years. By 2025, China alone will emit more carbon dioxide than the current combined total of the United States, Japan and

---

IMPACT ON CONSUMERS

In 2010 alone, the lost aggregate income (GDP) under the Clinton Administration's plan would be more than $227 billion (1992 dollars), $2,061 per household. Cumulatively, from 2001 to 2020, the loss of aggregate income per household would average almost $30,000....

Impact of Climate Change Policy on Consumers. ed. Charles E. Walker, et al. Washington, D.C.: American Council for Capital Formation, 1998.

Canada. Thus, while the United States and other developed countries would suffer serious economic dislocations, the economy of China and other less developed nations would continue to grow and the environment would not improve.

Agreeing to unilateral, binding CO_2 reductions would give American businesses one more reason to move production facilities overseas. This would entail a loss of jobs in both the service and high-wage manufacturing industries. It would seem foolish to reduce U.S. competitiveness and encourage the flight of America's industrial base to foreign countries.

UNFAIRLY PENALIZED

These results have not gone unnoticed, even within President Clinton's own party. In a letter to the President, six Democratic senators indicated that any climate change treaty that unfairly penalized the United States in relation to its trading partners or that was undertaken without an adequate assessment of the economic and social consequences of the pact would not achieve the necessary two-thirds vote in the Senate. In the end, any future global climate change commitments should be based on sound scientific evidence and a careful consideration of the economic and social costs involved. They should not be driven by questionable theories and value judgments made by unelected, unaccountable bureaucrats and environmental advocates.

PRUDENT CO₂ EMISSIONS CUTS MAKE ECONOMIC SENSE

Stephen J. DeCanio

Stephen J. DeCanio is an economist specializing in global environmental protection, energy and organization theory. He is the author of numerous books and scholarly articles. Formerly an Associate Professor at Yale, DeCanio is now Professor of Economics at the University of California - Santa Barbara.

■ POINTS TO CONSIDER

1. Explain the idea that climate change policy is a matter of risk management.

2. What are the estimates of direct damage with increased concentrations of carbon dioxide?

3. Contrast the "top-down" and "bottom-up" methods for estimating costs associated with reducing greenhouse gas emissions. Which method does the author favor and why?

4. Discuss the conclusions of the "bottom-up" studies cited.

Excerpted from the testimony of Stephen J. DeCanio before the Subcommittee on Energy and Environment of the U.S. House Committee on Science, October 9, 1997.

Special interest groups that seek to block action have made inflammatory and inaccurate statements suggesting that the cost of emissions reductions would be exorbitant.

Often economic analysis of an environmental policy issue uses ordinary cost-benefit analysis, and the criterion for decision is whether the directly measurable environmental benefits of the proposed pollution reduction are greater than the economic costs entailed. The case of climate change is different. Because of uncertainties in the magnitude, timing, and effects of climate change, the economic issue is more one of risk management than of straightforward cost-benefit comparison. The uncertainties associated with future climate change do not justify denial of the problem, but rather provide the most compelling rationale for beginning to act now to mitigate the risks and provide a reasonable margin of safety.

RISK MANAGEMENT

Climate change poses a massive public health problem, one no less worthy of policy attention and expenditure of resources than the control of infectious diseases or the suffering of aging. Indeed, given the links between climate and the spread of infectious diseases, these public health problems overlap.

Another risk created by climate change is the probable loss of species biodiversity, as environmental conditions and the characteristics of local habitats change more rapidly than species can adapt. The value of biodiversity includes potential medical compounds, the value of not foreclosing the options of future generations, the fact that predator/prey relationships (which would be disrupted by a loss of certain species) help control diseases spread by animal vectors, and the intrinsic worth of biological diversity.

The most common market response to protect against financial losses from uncertain events is to purchase insurance. Ordinary insurance markets work by spreading localized or individual risks over a large number of cases: actuarial statistics enable insurance providers to make a profit while paying claims when losses occur, thereby satisfying individuals' need for protection. But because climate change is global and some of the risks cover large areas or are planet-wide, this sort of insurance model does not apply.

The only way to purchase insurance against climate change is to make prudent investments now to avoid future dangers. We vaccinate our children against dangerous and potentially fatal diseases, even though there is a small monetary cost to the vaccinations and a slight risk of adverse reactions. The magnitude of the potential harm of life-threatening diseases such as polio, diphtheria, or measles is so great as to warrant the financial cost and health safety risks of inoculations. Undertaking policies to avoid environmental risks, even though there may be some cost associated with those policies, is at times the preferred course of action. There is undoubtedly broad and deep support in the United States for environmental protection measures that reduce the risks of illness and death from various pollutants.

DIRECT DAMAGES

In addition to protecting against the risks of climate change, policies to reduce greenhouse gas (GHG) emissions can also reduce some predictable damages from increasing global temperatures. Calculations of probable damages tend to take as their starting point the most firmly established consequences of global warming, such as rising sea levels, temperature-related changes in the demand for heating and air conditioning, health effects of increased temperature extremes, estimated changes in agricultural productivity, and water quality and availability. Current estimates of these potential damages are on the order of 1% to 2.5% of GDP for a doubling of atmospheric concentrations of CO_2.

The damage estimates reported above also do not assign a value to the risk of unpleasant surprises or catastrophic changes. By definition, the full dimensions of any such surprise cannot be known ahead of time, but three main types of potential climate catastrophe have been identified by the Intergovernmental Panel on Climate Change (IPCC). All are associated with non-linear responses to increases in atmosphere concentrations of greenhouse gases: (1) a runaway greenhouse effect, (2) disintegration of the West Antarctic Ice Sheet, and (3) structural changes in ocean currents.

The "runaway greenhouse effect" refers to a situation in which the warming from human GHG emissions begins to trigger additional emissions of GHGs from biological or mineralogical systems. This would lead to a rate of climate change much more rapid than suggested by current extrapolations.

DESTABILIZING FORCES

Even if the probability of any of these catastrophic possibilities is low, their risk value is high because the costs associated with them would be so huge. The need for prudent risk management comes to the forefront here; people are generally willing to pay to reduce the odds of unlikely but highly destructive events (residence fires, airplane crashes, nuclear power plant meltdowns). The cost of catastrophic outcomes, measured either as expected values or as people's willingness to pay to avoid risking them, has to be included in a complete accounting of the damages of climate change.

Finally, social and political systems would be threatened by the effects of climate change. Climate changes that reduce the habitability of low-lying coastal areas or island states could create large numbers of refugees. Forty percent of the U.S. population lives within 50 miles of the coast; it is estimated that half the world's population lives along ocean coastlines (Hanson and Lindh 1996). Similarly, if regional variations in rainfall patterns lead to desertification and localized famines, the number of climate refugees would be increased. Refugees are already a destabilizing factor in world politics, and large increases in their number would hardly contribute to peace. Because the effects of climate change would vary regionally, there is the possibility that international conflicts over water rights or other resources could be exacerbated. Climate change could destabilize domestic politics, even in democratic countries. Frightened populations might well be vulnerable to demagogic extremism in the event of an unexpected and painful climate crisis.

COSTS OF REDUCING GREENHOUSE GAS

A complete appraisal of measures to limit GHG emissions has to include both the benefits of avoiding the risks and damages described above as well as the price that would have to be paid to achieve those benefits by reducing emissions. Yet the political debate, at least in the United States, has tended to focus almost exclusively on the cost side of this calculation. Special interest groups that seek to block action have made inflammatory and inaccurate statements suggesting that the cost of emissions reductions would be exorbitant. For example, the Global Climate Coalition, an industry lobby group consistently opposed to U.S. commitment to binding restrictions on carbon emissions, recently

stated that a policy to reduce CO_2 emissions "would eliminate millions of American jobs, reduce America's ability to compete and force Americans into second-class lifestyles" (quotation reported in Brown 1996).

Economists employ two distinct methodologies for estimating the cost of reducing greenhouse gas emissions.

All of the commonly used top-down models are constructed in such a way as to include the assumption that reductions in greenhouse gas emissions can only be purchased at the expense of a reduction in the output of other goods and services. In all the top-down models, the various sectors and agents in the economy are presumed to be operating in a perfectly efficient manner, so that if an additional constraint is placed on their activities (such as being required to reduce emissions of greenhouse gases), the amount of ordinary goods and services that can be produced must fall.

Unlike the top-down studies, the bottom-up studies admit the possibility that some energy savings (and hence greenhouse gas reductions) could be achieved without loss to the larger economy.

LOSSES IN GDP

Even if the top-down modeling results are taken at face value, it is clear that the Gross Domestic Product (GDP) losses projected by these studies are hardly disastrous. A loss of one percent of GDP is not insignificant – it amounts to about \$70 billion (1992 dollars) per year at the current GDP level – yet it amounts to less than six months' of normal economic growth. That is, a permanent loss of one percent of GDP means only about a six months' delay in achieving any particular aggregate standard of living that would be reached in the ordinary course of economic growth.

Other considerations point to the conclusion that a proactive policy to reduce greenhouse gas emissions would not seriously disrupt the economy. Job reallocations caused by a reduction in fossil fuel use would be small relative to the average pace of job turnover. For example, the entire coal mining industry in the United States employed only 106,000 workers in 1995, down from 246,000 in 1980. Thus, this industry has been losing jobs at an average rate of just over 9,000 per year over the period 1980-95 without any GHG control measures in place (data from U.S. Bureau of the Census 1997, Table 654).

An alternative picture of the economic effects of GHG emissions abatement is given by the bottom-up studies. The IPCC surveyed the literature and found a large body of evidence that substantial emissions reductions could be accomplished at a net gain to the economy (IPCC 1996c). In the studies surveyed by the IPCC, an emissions reduction on the order of 25% from the base year level could be achieved at zero net average cost.

BOTTOM-UP STUDIES

Since publication of the IPCC report, several new studies estimating the positive economic potential of energy-efficiency improvements have appeared. The most comprehensive of these, *Scenarios of U.S. Carbon Reductions: Potential Impacts of Energy-Efficient and Low-Carbon Technologies by 2010 and Beyond,* was prepared by researchers at five of the national laboratories (Interlaboratory Working Group on Energy-Efficient and Low-Carbon Technologies 1997). This study examines four key sectors (buildings, transportation, industry, and electric utilities) in detail, and concludes that it would be possible to reduce carbon emissions to roughly 1990 levels by 2010 at "net costs to the U.S. economy…near or below zero in this time frame."

A second major new bottom-up study was carried out by a consortium of the Alliance to Save Energy, the American Council for an Energy-Efficient Economy, the Natural Resources Defense Council, the Tellus Institute, and the Union of Concerned

Scientists (1997). This report, titled *Energy Innovations: A Prosperous Path to a Clean Environment,* finds that the United States could follow an "Innovation Path" that by 2010 would lead to "a national energy system that, compared to the Present Path, reduces net costs by $530 per household, reduces global warming CO_2 emissions to ten percent below 1990 levels, and has substantially lower emissions of other harmful air pollutants." Finally, an adaptation of the U.S. Energy Information Agency's National Energy Modeling System (NEMS) model has been developed building in more dynamic assumptions about market transformation and behavioral change than originally contained in the NEMS model (Hoffman and Sylvan 1996). Running the NEMS model with these assumptions results in forecasts of GHG emissions in 2015 reduced by 13% to 39% from the NEMS baseline (the 39% reduction corresponds to a 21% reduction from 1990 emission levels), with a GDP gain of between 0.3% and 0.5%.

Companies and individuals around the world already are earning profitable returns by investing in energy-saving technologies such as modern fluorescent lighting systems, variable-speed motors, computer-controlled heating, ventilation, and air-conditioning systems (HVAC), new chlorofluorocarbon (CFC)-free refrigeration and cooling systems, and improved building design. Corporate leaders are increasingly recognizing the potential for earning money while making significant GHG reductions, as indicated by participation in voluntary energy-saving programs in the United States (such as the EPA's Green Lights and Energy Star initiatives, or the DOE/EPA Climate Wise program), and by the recent announcement by Keidanren, the multisector Japanese business group, to cut its CO_2 emissions 10%-20% from 1990 levels by 2010 (*Global Environmental Change Report* 1997).

CONCLUSION

Claims that meaningful GHG reduction measures would impose unacceptably high costs are exaggerated and fall outside the mainstream of economic thought. The key to minimizing the adjustments that will accompany the inevitable shift away from dependence on fossil fuels is to adopt a market-based GHG reduction strategy and speed up the development and adoption of the energy-efficient technologies of the future.

Alliance to Save Energy, American Council for an Energy-Efficient Economy, Natural Resources Defense Council, Tellus Institute, and Union of Concerned Scientists, 1997. **Energy Innovations: A Prosperous Path to a Clean Environment.** Washington, D.C.

Brown, Paul, 1996. "US and EU Seek Legal Curb on Gas Emissions," **The Guardian** (19 July).

Global Environmental Change Report, 1997. "Japanese Industry Vows CO_2 Reductions," Vol. 9, No. 5 (14 March): 6-7

Hanson, Hans, and Gunnar Lindh, 1996. "The Rising Risks of Rising Tides," **Forum for Applied Research and Public Policy** (Summer): 86-88.

Hoffman, John S., and Stephan D. Sylvan, 1996. "The Potential of Institutional, Organizational, and Technological Change to Improve the Future Productivity of the Energy Economy," unpublished manuscript.

Intergovernmental Panel of Climate Change, 1996c. **Climate Change 1995: Economic and Social Dimensions of Climate Change.** Contribution of Working Group III to the Second Assessment Report of the Intergovernmental Panel on Climate Change, Ed. James P. Bruce, Hoesung Lee, and Erik F. Haites. Cambridge: Cambridge University Press.

Interlaboratory Working Group on Energy-Efficient and Low-Carbon Technologies, 1997. **Scenarios of U.S. Carbon Reductions: Potential Impacts of Energy-Efficient and Low-Carbon Technologies by 2010 and Beyond.** U.S. Department of Energy, Office of Energy Efficiency and Renewable Energy.

U.S. Bureau of the Census, 1997. **Statistical Abstract of the United States: 1996.** Washington, D.C.

EXAMINING COUNTERPOINTS

This activity may be used as an individualized study guide for students in libraries and resource centers or as a discussion catalyst in small group and classroom discussions.

The Point

The Intergovernmental Panel on Climate Change, after viewing the body of evidence, has concluded that the balance of the evidence suggests that human activity has had an impact on climate. Public policy makers can no longer wait to enact laws and treaties to reduce carbon dioxide emission.

The Counterpoint

The scientific community has not reached a consensus about human activity's role in climate change. Hence, it would be unwise to negotiate treaties and craft legislation to reduce carbon dioxide emission, which would have the effect of slowing economic growth.

Guidelines

Part A

Examine the counterpoints above and then consider the following questions:

1. Do you agree more with the point or counterpoint? Why?

2. Which reading in this book best illustrates the point?

3. Which reading best illustrates the counterpoint?

4. Do any cartoons in this book illustrate the meaning of the point or counterpoint arguments? Which ones and why?

Part B

Social issues are usually complex, but often problems become oversimplified in political debates and discussions. Usually a polarized version of social conflict does not adequately represent the diversity of views that surround social conflicts. Examine the counterpoints. Then write down possible interpretations of this issue other than the two arguments stated in the counterpoints.

CHAPTER 2

WORLD ENVIRONMENT: UNDER CONTROL OR UNDER SIEGE?

READING

9

WATERS IN CRISIS: FISHING FOR PROFITS

A.V. Krebs

A.V. Krebs is editor and publisher of the Agbiz Tiller Online *(www.eal.com/tiller/). He is author of* The Corporate Reapers: The Book of Agribusiness *(Essential Books: 1992).*

■ POINTS TO CONSIDER

1. What are Individual Transferable Quotas (ITQs)? How have these affected rural fishing communities?

2. Discuss the parallel the author draws between agriculture and commercial fishing.

3. Why does the author end the article with the issue of waste?

Excerpted from Krebs, A.V. "Fishing for Profits: The Grim Reaper Casts His Net." **Progressive Populist.** Sept. 1998: 1, 12. Reprinted by permission.

Unlike in the past, where farmers and fishermen were the producers of our food, increasing numbers of them are now becoming simply the raw material providers for a giant food manufacturing system.

Just as the fundamental nature of American agriculture has been changed by corporate agribusiness, with factory-type farms, "vertical integration" and "forward contracting," where the processors control production, so has the world fishing industry been transformed by transnational corporate control, factory trawlers, value-added commercialism and Individual Transferable Quotas (ITQs).

ITQs

While corporate agribusiness has managed to successfully eliminate "excess human resources," that is, family farmers, from agriculture through a series of policies and price manipulations, the large corporations that today dominate seafood production are destroying this nation's fishing industry by promoting the privatization of the marine commons through the use of ITQs.

Under this system, participants, usually large corporate interests and in many cases the very same corporations that dominate corporate agribusiness, are allocated quota shares in the total annual catch of a given fishery. Quota holders can "transfer" – buy, sell, lease – shares on the open market, as with private property or futures contracts.

With each passing year it has become more apparent that the fate of the North Pacific fisheries industry need only to look at the demise of this nation's family farm system of agriculture in recent decades to fully comprehend its own fate. In each case capital has replaced efficiency and technology has replaced labor as corporate-controlled interests have become more intent on becoming "miners" of the land and seas rather than stewards of these natural and finite resources of the world's food supply.

STEWARDS NO LONGER

Unlike in the past, where farmers and fishermen were the producers of our food, increasing numbers of them are now becoming simply the raw material providers for a giant food manufacturing system.

Meanwhile, corporate food companies continue to seek to standardize our food supply through the "manufacturing" of our food, value-added food and creating "new" food through biotechnology while forcing consumers to pay a higher and higher quantitative and qualitative cost for their daily food.

By deifying "cost benefit analysis" at the expense of the "common good," these corporations have managed to annul the positive dimensions of the family farm system and the independent fisheries and eliminate their economic and environmental advantages, particularly as they relate to building genuine communities....

In his 1994 Congressional testimony Rolland Schmitten, assistant administrator for fisheries at the National Marine Fisheries Service, was asked the question "Do ITQs promote 'big business' as large companies have resources to buy or lease a significant amount of shares?" He replied: "This could happen, as experienced with grocery stores, agriculture and other enterprises .... To the extent that larger firms are relatively better capitalized, they may be able to obtain more shares relative to their needs for efficient operation than could smaller firms."

THREATENING SUSTAINABILITY

Despite such public rationalization, the corporate seafood industry's own spokespersons admit to the fact that the major problem facing an area such as the Alaskan groundfish fisheries is overcapitalization, abetted by heavy bank financing from abroad, principally Norway, and also by subsidies from the U.S. government.

As Vince Curry, president of the Pacific Seafood Processors Association, noted in 1994: "The problem with factory trawlers is they've built twice as many boats as have been justified, and they've created a very severe problem for this industry. They're driving ITQs because it was one way to take a public resource and use it to get them out of their bad investments."

Indeed, at the 21st Session of the Committee on Fisheries in Rome in 1995, the United Nations Food Agricultural Organization (FAO) Ministerial Conference, in adopting the Rome Consensus on World Fisheries, noted that the problem of overfishing in general, and overcapacity of industrial fishing fleets in particular, threatened the sustainability of the world's fisheries resources for present and future generations. They urged that governments and international organizations take prompt action to review the capacity of fishing

YEAR OF THE OCEANS

The deep ocean, it turns out, is far more varied and complex, far more important to the global ecosystem and far more threatened by humanity than most scientists ever dared imagine.

Fittingly, the United Nations has designated 1998 as the Year of the Ocean. The need for public understanding of the deep seas has never been greater....

Once thought to be a barren, inexhaustible sink, between 1946 and 1970, during the height of the Cold War, the U.S. dumped more than 47,000 barrels of nuclear waste into the Pacific Ocean...

As if the threats of undersea pollution were not enough, the creatures of the deep are also being attacked more directly. As traditional catches like haddock and cod are being harvested to near commercial extinction, fishermen are increasingly looking to exploit the biological riches of the deep....

Marc E. Norman. "The Year of the Oceans." **Earth Island Journal.** Spring 1998: 23.

---

fleets in relation to sustainable yields of fishery resources and where necessary reduce these fleets....

THREATENING COMMUNITIES

As in our country's rural communities, the growing crisis in our coastal fishing communities is systemic, for as it negatively affects the fishing fleet based in those communities so too does it impact the community's entire economy. Whereas previously the dollars earned from fishing multiplied as it moved through the community's economy, now that money is either no longer being generated or, in the case of the large transnationals, it leaves the community immediately on being monetized.

For example, in 1992 Sealaska, the regional Native corporation for southeast Alaska, commissioned a report about the socioeconomic impacts of the halibut and sablefish quota programs which placed the quotas in the context of past limited-entry measures. Restrictions associated with these measures, Greenpeace's Jed Greer reports, have reduced rural communities' access to fishing grounds, particularly in the halibut fishery where residents were active participants.

With very low per-capita income levels, the report explains, individuals or households of these communities would find it difficult to purchase quota. They were also likely to sell their shares out of necessity, frequently to higher-income, urban-based fishers. Since a limited-entry program for salmon fisheries began in 1975, by way of illustration, the number of salmon permits owned by rural residents of southeast Alaska had declined by 60% in the ensuing 17 years....

AGRIBUSINESS MODEL

Taking a page from corporate agribusiness's book, the giants of the fishing industry have in many ways duplicated those conditions which have been the hallmark agriculture's "harvest of shame" – the treatment of its migratory labor force.

Like corporate agribusiness, factory trawler companies have also been using lax labor laws to maintain their operations, resulting in the fact that shipbuilding jobs have not been going to American shipyard workers; factory trawler workers have been excluded from federal minimum wage and overtime laws while some make no money at all; crews are often cheated out of wages and these workers have less rights to file wage claims. At the same time trawler companies have a history of opposing labor unions, and they usually do not hire local workers but frequently hire foreign workers....

CONCLUSION

In 1994 alone, North Pacific factory trawlers threw overboard more than 581 million pounds of dead and dying fish because they were the wrong size, sex or species. The waste from these 60 factory trawlers was greater than all the similar fish caught and kept by all fishing vessels in the Northeast U.S. during that same year.

Thus, as our nation's small fisheries are becoming subsumed in the hulls of giant corporate factory trawlers, they are joining those thousands of family farmers who already have been lost to corporate agribusiness' grim reapers.

READING

10

WATERS IN CRISIS: FISHING FOR SOLUTIONS

Michael DeAlessi

Michael DeAlessi is a Research Associate for the Competitive Enterprise Institute (CEI). He is also Coordinator for the Center for Private Conservation. The following reading is adapted from a more in-depth analysis of free-market approaches to marine conservation published by the environment unit of the Institute of Economic Affairs in London.

■ **POINTS TO CONSIDER**

1. How would the author respond to claims that the fishing industry is dying?

2. What role do private property rights play in marine resource management?

3. Discuss the author's view of Individual Transferable Quotas (ITQs). Contrast his view with that of the previous author.

DeAlessi, Michael. "Fishing for Solutions." **CEI Update.** March 1998: 8. Reprinted with permission, Competitive Enterprise Institute (CEI).

Reports of the death of fishing have been exaggerated.

While dramatic stories of the depletion of the world's fish stocks frequently grab the spotlight in the popular press, reports of the death of fishing have been exaggerated. Stock of some species of fish, however, have been seriously depleted and others are certainly in danger due to poor management regimes around the world. As long as fishery managers and policy makers fail to recognize just why these problems exist, both fish stocks and the people who depend on them will suffer.

OBSERVING SUCCESS

Unfortunately, examples of successful fisheries conservation are frequently overlooked, and any institutional analysis of fisheries management around the world is rare. It is instructive, therefore, to examine the means by which individuals can be encouraged to manage marine resources sustainably, in particular within the framework of the economics of property rights.

In the absence of any private rights to marine resources, there is little if any incentive to conserve resources, and fisheries suffer. When any fish left in the sea are likely to simply wind up in someone else's net, conservation measures are frequently ignored and difficult to enforce. The Common Fisheries Policy of the European Union is one of the most egregious examples of management gone wrong – fishing quotas are allocated politically and rarely reduced, even in the face of irrefutable declines in fish stocks. There is also a burgeoning market for illegally caught fish and inadvertently caught fish are commonly caught and discarded, likely dead.

SETTING LIMITS

On the other hand, where fishers are able to collectively determine overall catches for themselves, they have strong incentives to ensure that their harvests are sustainable and that their limits are enforced. Limiting access and allowing the private ownership of fishery resources, or at least some sense of it, is the surest way to ensure the long-term health of a fishery. Thus, the institutional arrangements – that is, the set of rules that govern a fishery – are the single most important indicators of the health of fish stocks around the world. The closer these institutional arrangements resemble private property rights, held either in common or individually, the better off a fisher tends to be. This holds true from communal

arrangements among villagers in the South Pacific to capital-
intensive, deep-sea fisheries in New Zealand.

Allowing groups or individuals to own resources in the oceans is
the ideal solution, but in cases where this is not a feasible reform,
privatizing access rights has also proven effective. One such exclusive access right is the Individual Transferable Quota (ITQ), a transferable right to harvest fish. New Zealand is particularly noteworthy
for its experiment with ITQs, which has transformed fishing thereby
creating incentives to demand more sustainable catch levels and by
reducing incentives for political wrangling over resources.

STEP IN THE RIGHT DIRECTION

ITQ systems are not free-market solutions, but they have
improved fisheries management in many cases by successfully
introducing market mechanisms that encourage conservation. In
spite of their flaws, ITQs are a step in the right direction, and in
the case of New Zealand, have even started to evolve into real
private property rights.

Exclusive ownership rights to resources also create incentives to
develop and use technology both to protect resources and to
increase their production. Stronger rights create stronger incentives
for conservation and stewardship. For example, in Japan, fishery
cooperatives own rights to fish in coastal waters. They not only conserve and protect their resources but strive to enhance their fisheries
by sinking artificial reefs that both attract and propagate species.

A pragmatic reform, not only in Europe but in the United States
and Canada, would be to follow the New Zealand model; to
introduce a system of ITQs and allow the owners of ITQs to
collectively set appropriate catch levels and to otherwise begin to
manage the fisheries themselves.

OZONE APOCALYPSE HAS COME AND GONE

Ben Lieberman

Ben Lieberman is an environmental research associate with the Competitive Enterprise Institute (CEI). His work on stratospheric ozone depletion and the Montreal Protocol was published in the spring of 1994 in The Buffalo Environmental Law Journal. *CEI is a nonprofit public policy group which promotes free enterprise and limited government. Contact CEI at 1001 Connecticut Avenue, NW, Suite 1250, Washington, D.C. 20036; www.cei.org/.*

■ POINTS TO CONSIDER

1. Describe the framing of ozone depletion in the media, according to the reading.

2. What political reaction did ozone depletion inspire?

3. According to the author, how many ozone predictions materialized?

4. Summarize the myths, delineated by Lieberman, of health and environment risks due to ozone depletion.

Lieberman, Ben. "Ozone Apocalypse Has Come and Gone." **Human Events.** April 25, 1997: 17. Reprinted with permission.

Now, five years and billions of dollars in additional research later, we know how many of these dire predictions have come true.

The scariest media event in the history of environmentalism turned out to be a false alarm.

On February 3, 1992, NASA called an unscheduled, "emergency" press conference to announce the imminent threat of an ozone hole over the Arctic region. Scientist James G. Anderson said that the risk was "a good solid eight" out of ten that an ozone hole similar to the ones seen annually over Antarctica would soon appear in the North.

He also predicted Arctic ozone holes in future years. "We're not concerned with just remote areas now," added Dr. Michael Kurylo. "What we're dealing with extends to very populated regions in the Northern Hemisphere." "Everybody should be alarmed about this; it's far worse than we thought," he emphasized.

PRESS PREDICTED CATASTROPHE

The press had a field day, reporting the news as if the earth were about to be hit by a biblical plague. Nearly every major newspaper, news magazine and network news program ran lurid stories predicting substantial increases in skin cancer, cataracts, even AIDS, as well as catastrophic declines in crop yields and destruction of the ocean food chain, all caused by the presumed increase in ultraviolet B radiation (UVB) penetrating the now-damaged ozone shield. *Time* magazine was perhaps the most hysterical among the major media, turning the press conference into a cover story, which, among other things, declared that "life may never be the same."

In Washington, D.C., the undisputed master of Arctic ozone hole disaster was Al Gore. The then-senator from Tennessee repeated all of the above prognostications and added a few of his own, including "blind rabbits in our back yards."

Three days after the press conference, Gore described the "immediate, acute emergency threat," to his colleagues on the Senate floor. And in a vicious, and effective, attack against George Bush, he claimed that the ozone hole could conceivably open up over the President's summer residence. "Now, with the potential ozone hole above Kennebunkport, the message is beginning to get

Cartoon by Henry Payne. Reprinted with permission, **UFS.**

through," he wryly noted.

Swayed by Gore's logic, the Senate voted 96 to zero to move up from the year 2000 to the end of 1995 the existing phaseout of chlorofluorocarbons (CFCs), the class of refrigerants believed to cause the damage. On February 11, a mere eight days after the press conference, a beleaguered President Bush agreed to the acceleration.

PREDICTIONS

Fast forward to 1997. Now, five years and billions of dollars in additional research later, we know how many of these dire predictions have come true.

Absolutely none of them.

First, the 1992 Arctic ozone hole never materialized, though NASA's quiet retraction several months later was ignored by many of the same journalists and Tennessee senators who made such a big deal out of the original prediction.

The retraction did nothing to reverse the acceleration of the CFC phaseout, a move that is already costing car air-conditioner owners a fortune. Nor have any Arctic ozone holes opened up in subsequent years. And, to George and Barbara's relief, NASA scientist Arlin Krueger noted that "there has never been an ozone hole over Kennebunkport, and I don't really expect one."

Obviously, the parade of horribles attributed to the Arctic ozone hole have not come to pass either. But this would be so even if a hole did open up.

Most of the claims of harm to human health and the environment linked to the imaginary Arctic ozone hole were simply repeats of the anecdotal evidence of damage blamed on its real Antarctic counterpart, a phenomenon that has been detected since 1979.

OZONE HORRIBLES A MYTH

But scientific research has shown that the widely publicized stories of increases in skin cancer, eye damage and the rest are a myth. In the only epidemiologic study of the Antarctic ozone hole's effects, a team of Johns Hopkins scientists concluded that there is "no convincing evidence to support the reported acute adverse health effects."

This did not surprise the researchers, as the annualized increase in UVB exposure due to an ozone hole is "in the region of one percent," far too little to cause the predicted catastrophes. "UVB increases naturally by about 5,000% between pole and equator, largely because of the change in the average angle of the sun," says University of Virginia physicist Fred Singer.

Thus, the increased UVB in the Antarctic (or Arctic) due to an ozone hole is still far less than in most of the rest of the world, and the one percent rise is equivalent to a permanent move of less than ten miles towards the tropics.

So why all the exaggeration? The passage of time has also revealed the answer. Almost everyone involved in the scare gained something from it. NASA's press conference worked wonders for its funding levels – whatever the state of the ozone layer, there is certainly no hole in ozone research spending. The media got a sensational story. And politicians were able to claim that they saved their constituents from Armageddon.

Little wonder we're seeing the same *modus operandi* in the context of global warming.

It's probably too late to reverse the policy errors, but the facts,

OZONE'S LESSON

The hysteria, which accelerated after the 1985 discovery of the so-called Antarctic ozone hole, led to the Montreal Protocol, culminating in a total ban on CFC production among developed nations by January 1, 1996. The cost has been and will continue to be substantial, perhaps as much as $100 billion in the U.S. alone....

Ben Lieberman. "Ozone Depletion's Lesson." **CEI Update.** Sept. 1998: 6.

however belatedly they come out, are still important. And the facts are that the feared Arctic ozone hole never occurred, and even if it had it would not have been a crisis.

Time was wrong – life is pretty much the same. It just costs a lot more to get your car air-conditioner fixed.

READING

12

A SKY FULL OF HOLES

Janet S. Wager

Janet S. Wager wrote the following article in her capacity as editor of Nucleus, *a quarterly publication of the Union of Concerned Scientists (UCS). UCS is a citizen/scientist organization which promotes stewardship of the global environment, renewable energy, sustainable agriculture, and curtailment of weapons of mass destruction. Contact UCS at Two Brattle Square, Cambridge, MA 02238, www.ucsusa.org/.*

■ **POINTS TO CONSIDER**

1. Summarize the claims the author makes about ozone depletion.

2. Discuss ozone, the ozone layer, and how the ozone layer is depleted.

3. What criticisms does the author have of "ozone skeptics?"

4. Explain the efforts to curb ozone depletion.

Excerpted from Wager, Janet S. "Double Exposure." **Nucleus.** Winter 1995-6: 1-3, 12. Reprinted with permission.

The vast majority of the scientific community agrees that a hole in the ozone layer has opened over the Antarctic every austral spring since the late 1970s.

On January 1, 1996, the world's industrial countries must stop producing chlorofluorocarbons (CFCs), carbon tetrachloride, and methyl chloroform – three of the human-made chemicals that are destroying the Earth's protective ozone layer. This treaty-mandated production ban comes not a moment too soon. By the beginning of October, when the hole in the ozone layer over Antarctica had reached its seasonal peak, it had grown to over 8.1 million square miles – more than twice the size of Canada – and had expanded at a record rate, according to the UN's World Meteorological Organization.

CONFIRMED OZONE HOLE

The vast majority of the scientific community agrees that a hole in the ozone layer has opened over the Antarctic every austral spring since the late 1970s, permitting harmful ultraviolet radiation to reach the Earth; that this ultraviolet radiation will lead to various human health problems and damage to plants and animals; that the hole is caused by human-made ozone-destroying chemicals; and that ozone depletion is occurring at all latitudes (except the tropics) during all seasons.

In fact, the scientific consensus is so broad that the 1995 Nobel Prize in chemistry – an award given only to those whose research has been widely accepted by the mainstream scientific community – was awarded to the three scientists who discovered that human-made chemicals can damage the Earth's ozone layer.

THE SCIENCE

Within the stratosphere (upper atmosphere), ozone (O_3) is a rare gas that is principally concentrated in a band that extends from an altitude of nine to 22 miles above Earth. This ozone "layer" is extremely important for life on the planet, since ozone absorbs certain ultraviolet lightwaves (UV-B), which, if they reached the Earth in great quantities, would be biologically harmful. (Ozone is also present in the troposphere, the lower atmosphere, where it is the main component of smog.)

The science of stratospheric ozone depletion is well known.

When molecules of normal oxygen (O_2) are struck by high-energy light rays, these molecules break down into two oxygen (O) atoms. Ozone is formed when one of those atoms combines with another molecule of O_2. In this case, explains Union of Concerned Scientists (UCS) Staff Scientist Darren Goetze, "three is indeed a crowd. Ozone is not a particularly stable molecule, and it can be broken down by ultraviolet light rays, as well as by chemical reactions with various naturally occurring compounds."

FRAGILE EQUILIBRIUM

"The two opposite processes of synthesis and destruction and the factors that contribute to them produce an overall dynamic equilibrium that leaves a small net residual amount of ozone in the atmosphere," says Goetze. "And it is a very small amount for every ten million molecules of air; for example, two million are oxygen of the type we breathe, but only three molecules are ozone." Unfortunately, the equilibrium has been disturbed in the last 50 years by the human contribution of ozone-destroying chemicals to the atmosphere. These chemicals include sources of chlorine (such as chlorofluorocarbons, carbon tetrachloride, and methyl chloroform) and bromine (from such compounds as methyl bromide), as well as oxides of nitrogen from fossil fuel burning.

CFCs alone are responsible for 80 percent of total human-caused atmospheric ozone depletion. "These compounds are so effective at destroying ozone," explains Goetze, "because chlorine is highly reactive with ozone. But the chlorine itself is not altered or destroyed in the reaction. In fact, one chlorine atom can react with up to 100,000 ozone molecules before it forms a chemically stable compound and diffuses out of the atmosphere."

Bromine is an even more effective ozone destroyer. "Not only does it react with ozone, says Goetze, "but it speeds up the reactions that liberate chlorine atoms as well. The result is that an atom of bromine destroys at least 40 times more ozone than does an atom of chlorine."

Unfortunately, the destruction of the ozone layer will continue for many years, even with a production ban. The chemicals already emitted into the atmosphere from human activities will remain there for decades, continuing to destroy the ozone layer before it begins to recover. And recovery is only possible if countries adhere to the production ban.

THE SKEPTICS

Even with the weight of science – evidence that has been reviewed and accepted by literally thousands of experts around the world – some people still claim that ozone depletion is not a serious problem. According to Nancy Cole, project manager for UCS's Sound Science Initiative, the current challenge to the scientific consensus on the ozone problem is coming primarily from "a few credentialed scientists affiliated with influential conservative think tanks that are pushing an extreme anti-regulatory agenda...."

In its rush to wipe out environmental regulations, Congress seems to be listening to the skeptics and ignoring mainstream scientists. An article in the *New York Times* reported, for example, that during a committee hearing Representative Tom DeLay admitted that he had not read the peer-reviewed, authoritative report on ozone depletion prepared by the World Meteorological Organization, but that he had only seen the work of people like Fred Singer, one of the most vocal of the skeptics.

THE SOLUTIONS

Current skepticism notwithstanding, the history of international action to address ozone depletion is impressive. As early as 1977, the United Nations Environment Programme (UNEP) held a meeting on the ozone problem and recommended a world plan of action. That same year, the United States hosted an intergovernmental meeting to discuss international controls on CFCs, and the U.S. Congress passed an ozone protection amendment to the Clean Air Act.

In 1981 the UNEP Governing Council recommended formulating an international treaty to protect the ozone layer, and over the next few years negotiators hammered out an agreement. In 1985 representatives from 43 countries adopted the Vienna Convention for the Protection of the Ozone Layer. Although it did not commit the signatory nations to phasing out use of suspected ozone-destroying chemicals, it was nevertheless a significant achievement....

During the next several years, the international community took concrete steps to phase out ozone-depleting substances as evidence mounted that ozone was actually being lost in the stratosphere. In 1987, 37 nations signed the Montreal Protocol on Substances That Deplete the Ozone Layer, agreeing to limit their

Cartoon by David Catrow. Reprinted with permission, **Copley New Service.**

release of CFCs and halons (certain chemicals that contain bromine) and to halve CFC emissions by the year 2000, with some exceptions given to developing countries.

STRENGTHENING PROTOCOLS

The Protocol was revised and strengthened in 1990 and then again in 1992. The 1990 revisions required industrial countries to phase out CFCs and halons completely by 2000 and developing countries to do so by 2010, and the Protocol was extended to include carbon tetrachloride and methyl chloroform. In 1992, delegates from over 90 countries moved forward the cutoff dates for CFCs, carbon tetrachloride, and methyl chloroform to 1996, and halons to 1994. They also agreed that there should be controls on and an eventual phaseout of the hydrochlorofluorocarbons (HCFCs) that would be used as substitutes for CFCs. In addition, production of methyl bromide was to be frozen at 1991 levels in 1995. These various agreements all have the status of formal treaties in international law....

The various international agreements and laws related to ozone depletion received strong bipartisan support in this country when initially enacted, even though some industry groups and politicians opposed restrictions on the production and use of ozone-depleting chemicals. With the 1994 election of a Republican congressional majority, however, these opponents have a greater opportunity to

REVERSING TRENDS

Measurements by scientists at National Oceanic and Atmospheric Aministration's (NOAA) Climate Monitoring and Diagnostics Laboratory in Boulder, Colo., indicate that three bromine-containing fire extinguishants, halons H-1211, H-1301 and H-2402 are still being released into the atmosphere in crucial amounts....

Scientists are concerned about the increase in halons because bromine, an element in the halons, is 50 times more efficient at depleting ozone in the atmosphere than its nearest rival, chlorine, a component in chlorofluorocarbons (CFCs), and because the gases last a long time in the atmosphere.

By the year 2005, if halons continue to increase in the atmosphere, the total amount of equivalent chlorine (chlorine + bromine) will no longer be decreasing as we observed a few years ago. This could cause the recovery of the ozone layer to slow down....

"Some Ozone-Depleting Chemicals Continue to Increase in Atmosphere." Feb. 20, 1998 Press Release of the U.S. National Oceanic and Atmospheric Administration.

try to delay phaseout timetables. Through the budgeting process, Congress is also seeking to weaken implementation of the Montreal Protocol, and it now appears likely that financial assistance previously promised to developing countries to help them implement a CFC phaseout will be sharply reduced.

GOOD FAITH

The preservation and recovery of the stratospheric ozone layer depends on good faith implementation and vigorous enforcement of the Montreal Protocol's provisions by all signatory nations. Through the Sound Science Initiative, UCS is working to make sure that the voices of scientists around the country will be heard as legislators set policy on dealing with stratospheric ozone depletion.

13

POPULATION GROWTH: THE MARKET SOLUTION

Richard L. Stroup and Jane S. Shaw

Richard L. Stroup is Professor of Economics at Montana State University and Senior Associate at the Political Economy Research Center (PERC) in Bozeman, Montana. He is coauthor with James Gwartney of Economics: Private and Public Choice. *Jane S. Shaw is Senior Associate at PERC. PERC is a nonprofit organization that explores market solutions to environmental problems. Shaw previously served as Associate Economics Editor of* Business Week.

■ POINTS TO CONSIDER

1. What is the significance of Thomas Malthus' work?

2. Describe the difference between the "apocalyptics" and the "cornucopians."

3. How do the authors explain contemporary famines?

4. Explain, from the authors' point of view, the reason for decreasing birth rates.

5. Identify the connection between private property and population growth.

Societies based on private property rights and markets can support many people because private property rights allow for innovation and reward it, while penalizing wastefulness.

Fear of population growth has been with us for a long time. Thomas Malthus forecast disaster from population growth in An *Essay on the Principles of Population,* published in 1798. He argued that higher wages would lead to higher birth rates, and that population increases would drive wages down toward a subsistence level. Thus, for most people, life would be a constant battle against starvation.

TECHNOLOGY

But Malthus did not foresee the impact of technology, which has loosened nature's grip on our ability to produce food. Today, pesticides, machines, refrigeration, and other advances make it possible to feed enormous numbers of people very well. Except in cases fostered by war and political repression, starvation is rarely a widespread problem these days, and in advanced nations, obesity is a far greater threat to health than starvation. Life expectancy in the developed countries has nearly doubled, from 40 years to well over 70 years now.

As human knowledge and skills grew, resources changed their character. Petroleum was simply a gooey, smelly substance when people encountered it in Pennsylvania in the middle of the 19th century. But human ingenuity (pushed along by the fact that whale oil, a key source of fuel for lighting, was becoming scarce) turned petroleum into a source of fuel. The "goo" became a valuable resource.

Was Malthus fundamentally wrong? Or was he right before his time? Today an active debate is going on between the "apocalyptics" and the "cornucopians." Apocalyptics are modern-day Malthusians who believe that technical innovation has only temporarily stayed catastrophe. Cornucopians are optimists who believe that progress will continue.

THE BEAT GOES ON

The apocalyptics continue to claim that famine is around the corner. Paul Ehrlich predicted in 1968 that "in the 1970s...

hundreds of millions of people are going to starve to death." That didn't happen, but the drumbeat continues. "Scores of countries with rapid population growth – among them Iran, Egypt, Ethiopia, Nigeria, and Mexico – will find themselves facing huge food deficits in the years ahead," said Lester Brown in the Worldwatch Institute's 1995 report, *State of the World*. Interestingly, such projections assume the end of important technical advances, but not the end of population growth pressures.

The apocalyptics have a point. Population growth has accelerated during the 20th century. Between 1850 and 1900, world population grew at an annual rate of 0.6 percent. By 1970, it was growing at a rate of 2.06 percent, far faster than at any time in history. Furthermore, prosperity is not universal, by any means. In some countries, such as Ethiopia, there has been mass starvation. Disasters can and do occur, and progress is not guaranteed or automatic.

HISTORY ON OUR SIDE

But the cornucopians have the experience of recent decades, even centuries of history, on their side. Every projection of inevitable or global doom has, up to now, been proven wrong. Technical advances have allowed more and more people not only to be fed, but to become increasingly well off. Even a person living at the poverty level in the United States, for example, is able to spend more now, in real terms, than the average person's income in the United States in 1960.

Widespread starvation today always grows out of political conflict. Ethiopia has some of the best farmland in Africa, but political disruptions have thrown food production there into a tailspin. The difficulties include on-going civil war, resources directed largely by central government decision makers rather than private owners, and large amounts of land taken from the control of some groups and handed over to others. In such a situation, population growth can be a disaster. But population growth is not the source of the problem.

Furthermore, it is unlikely that growth in world population will continue at the rates we have seen in our lifetime. Some demographers now surmise that the rapid population growth in the 20th century is a unique phenomenon reflecting, in part, our enormous success in reducing mortality rates. Lower birth rates have lagged behind these dramatic declines in mortality rates.

DECREASING BIRTH RATES

Now birth rates are going down, too. Between 1970 and 1990, the population growth rate declined from a frightening 2.06 percent to 1.73 percent. Fertility rates were falling all over the world. In Thailand the fertility rate fell from 4.6 children per woman in 1975 to 2.3 children in 1987; in Colombia, it fell from 4.7 in 1976 to 2.8 in 1990. Declines like this are widespread in the developing world. And in the industrialized countries at current birth rates, the population is barely replacing itself.

The full explanation for these declines is complex and not fully understood. But the low birth rates in the industrial world seem pretty clearly linked to economic growth.

Consider this: In developing countries, the benefits of having children are much greater than the costs to parents. The costs of rearing children are low, since families do not invest heavily in children's schooling or health care, and children can often contribute income to the family while they are young. Mothers do not have many opportunities to earn income outside the home, so the opportunity cost of staying home is low.

In the industrialized world, however, expectations for children's achievements are much higher. Families invest heavily in their children's education, and their children may not earn any income for decades. Furthermore, most women have attained an education that opens up opportunities for earning income outside the home; staying home with many children therefore means giving up substantial income. In other words, in the more specialized world of the industrial West, it is costly to rear children. As you would expect, then, there is a trend away from having many children in the Western countries.

This shift to lower birth rates in the West is called the "Demographic Transition." As economic growth transforms the developing world, we expect the same transition to occur there, provided that opportunities for women's education continue to open up, and investment in children's education proves valuable.

THE MALTHUSIAN ERROR

In their argument with the Malthusians, then, the cornucopians have the edge. But the cornucopians are wrong if they assume that the progress that has occurred in the past will inevitably continue. In assessing the impact of population growth, we must remember that it is the institutions that matter, not the rate of population growth itself. Those institutions may be more fragile than some cornucopians think.

An essay by the late economist F.A. Hayek helps to put population growth and institutions into perspective. In *The Fatal Conceit,* Hayek explained that Malthus had a point. In Malthus' day, people were relatively homogeneous as laborers, so that adding more workers to a given economy might well have led to diminishing returns. But over time, as a complex market society developed and expanded, specialization of labor allowed people to provide unique contributions. New individuals began to add greater value than diminishing amounts of value. This additional value made possible more production of food and other goods and services, enabling many more people to live on Earth.

Says Hayek: "Human population grew in a sort of chain reaction in which greater density of occupation of territory tended to produce new opportunities for specialization and thus led to an increase of individual productivity and in turn to a further increase of numbers."

PRIVATE PROPERTY

This process occurred however, Hayek makes clear, only because of private property rights, which provide the basis for trade and specialization. Where private property rights are the norm, as in industrial nations most of the time, high population densities can easily be supported. Even a nation as densely populated as the Netherlands (which has 931 people per square mile, compared with India's 658 people per square mile) has no trouble feeding itself. In fact, it is an agricultural exporter. James Gwartney, Robert Lawson, and Walter Block in their new book *Economic Freedom of the World: 1975-1995* have demonstrated that the freedom to own and trade property rights strongly influences both the level and growth of prosperity among nations.

Societies based on private property rights and markets can support many people because private property rights allow for innovation and reward it, while penalizing wastefulness. Resource users must pay for what they use, so they have an incentive to

HIGH-YIELD FARMING

The Sahel is about one million square miles of sparsely-populated arid land that lies to the south of the Sahara Desert. Its very name means "edge of the desert...."

The Sahel suffered hundreds of thousands of famine deaths after "The Population Bomb" was published – and there would have been more, except that the region is home to only 0.0009 percent of the world's population. High-yield farming has never been tried there. However, research has just developed a new drought-tolerant hybrid sorghum that shows real promise....

Dennis T Avery. "Halting Population Growth Won't Save the Environment." **The Bridge News**. Jan. 10, 1997.

reduce their costs and increase the attractiveness of their products to increase their sales. The result is not simply more production but also savings in resources. A continuing process of innovation leads continually to a more efficient economy that takes ever greater advantage of the skills of more and more human beings. Economist Mikhail Bernstam has shown, for example, that in the 1980s (before the collapse of Communism), countries with market-based economies used only about one third as much energy and steel per unit of output as the socialist nations used. Without a system of private property rights, the socialist countries were extremely wasteful.

PROSPERITY IS PRO-ENVIRONMENT

The prosperity resulting from property rights and market institutions also has desirable environmental effects. As incomes grow, the demand for environmental quality grows even faster. Donald Coursey of the University of Chicago has found that people who are ten percent richer are willing and able to spend 25 percent more on environmental quality. That means that wealthier people want to protect the environment, and are able to take action to do so. This may take different forms, including the passage of laws, insistence on protection through the courts, and the willingness to pay more for clean, pollution-free property.

Unfortunately, many people today live in countries where government control of property discourages wise use of resources and hampers the specialization that makes people prosperous, stabilizes population, and makes it possible to support high population densities without ruining the environment. Where private property is not protected, people are not allowed to reap what they sow – or otherwise benefit from what they produce. In these situations, population expansion makes it hard for people to live decently. If those countries could adopt and protect the institution of private property and market institutions, the picture would be far different, as it is in Singapore and Hong Kong, for example. These are tiny places with minimal natural resources, yet they support large populations. Indeed, in India, where the government recently loosened its control of property, food production has soared and the famines of the past have become only a memory.

CONCLUSION

In the debate between the apocalyptics and the cornucopians, economists award the victory to the cornucopians. Greater population does not have to be a problem. But the apocalyptics have a warning that we should heed: If the institutions that shape the economy are wrong, we may have a population crisis after all.

READING

14

POPULATION GROWTH: THE MARKET DISASTER

Emanuel Sferios

Emanuel Sferios is a social justice advocate living in Berkeley, California. Currently a graduate student, he is active in a variety of grassroots campaigns, from hunger issues to immigrant rights.

■ POINTS TO CONSIDER

1. Who is Paul Ehrlich?

2. How are consumers and producers a part of the population problem?

3. Discuss the role of economic globalization in population growth.

4. Identify the means by which the author believes population growth will slow.

Excerpted from Sferios, Emanuel. "Population, Immigration and the Environment." **Z Magazine.** June 1998: 24-9. Reprinted with permission.

Overpopulation, environmental degradation, and social injustice all result from the same global economic system that seeks to increase profits at all costs.

...While most environmentalists today agree that profit-seeking corporations and government policy play a critical role in the environmental crisis, many still harbor oversimplified notions that population growth, if not a direct cause of environmental degradation, is nevertheless the main ecological threat. Ever since the publication in 1968 of Paul Ehrlich's *The Population Bomb,* this notion has slowly increased in popularity. The image of a run-away population "explosion" exceeding the earth's "carrying capacity" and leading to ecological devastation has a certain dramatic appeal, yet adds little to the formation of effective strategies for ecological sustainability. It also does much to foment racist, anti-immigrant sentiments.

POPULATION PROBLEM

The debate focuses almost exclusively on absolute numbers of people, ignoring the varying environmental impacts of different social institutions and classes. Charts and graphs depicting "out-of-control" population growth replace research analysis on exactly which people, where, are affecting the environment, and how. The impact of an immigrant family, for example, living in a one-bedroom apartment and using mass transit pales in comparison to that of a wealthy family living in a single family home with a swimming pool and two cars. "The average Swiss," points out Walden Bello, former director of Food First, "pours 2,000 times more toxic waste into the environment than the average Sahelian farmer." The U.S. is home to five percent of the world's population yet consumes 30 percent of the world's resources, and with the richest 1.1 billion people on the planet consuming 64 percent of the wealth and the poorest 1.1 billion just two percent, it makes little sense to blame population as a whole for today's environmental crisis.

Despite the fact that the wealthy consume far greater resources than the poor, it is not consumers, but producers – and the social institutions in which they operate – which account for the vast majority of environmental degradation. Most consumers have little control over industrial production and consumption decisions, and most industrial production and consumption decisions are made with little regard for population levels. The military, for example, is the nation's largest single polluter, and it does so regardless of the number of people who happen to be living. U.S. transnational corporations are aggressively marketing to increase consumption in countries like Mexico and China who have large populations yet have traditionally been low per capita consumers. As Santos Gomez, member of Political Ecology Group (PEG) organizing board states, "consumption varies far more widely as a function of marketing than the absolute numbers of people, or even individual consumer choices." Only if one believes the *laissez-faire* notion that supply merely fills demand (including a demand for nuclear weapons, we presume, and answering machines designed to break down after 500 uses) can one blame consumers for the environmental degradation resulting from industrial production.

POPULATION DENSITY

Even land development has little to do with population growth. Sprawling suburbs in the U.S. which gobble up prime agricultural land and wildlife habitat are planned and built by developers for the sake of profits and are increasing six times faster than the population. Population density also has no impact on the environment *per se*. Holland, for example, is one of the most densely populated countries in the world, with 4,500 people per 1,000 hectares. It is also one of the most ecologically strong, devoting ten percent of its land to ecological protection. Compare this to Brazil with only 170 people per 1,000 hectares and an unprecedented rate of rainforest destruction and it becomes clear that corporate and government policy, not population density, accounts for environmentalist degradation. In the U.S. many environmentalists are actually calling for greater population density with improved mass transit, thus reducing suburban sprawl and the need for automobiles.

The notion that higher population equals greater demand, however, and that individual consumer choice fuels production, are basic assumptions underlying the arguments of anti-population-growth environmentalists....

This is not to say that choosing a more environmentally and socially responsible lifestyle is unimportant, but only that consumer choices have marginal impact on the production decisions which really impact the environment, and over which the public has little control. In fact, many corporate actions significantly restrict the public's ability to choose more sustainable lifestyles. In the 1930s and 1940s, for example, General Motors, Firestone, and Standard Oil (now Chevron) bought out and dismantled the electric trolley system in Los Angeles and 100 other cities in order to guarantee demand for their products. Compared to the rail system in Europe, our highway-intensive transportation system is but one example of how powerful corporate decisions make it difficult for many people to choose a life of voluntary simplicity.

The above examples are meant to demonstrate that in a system driven by profit fewer people in no way insures less environmental impact. Likewise, more people in no way implies greater impact. This is not to imply that numbers of people should be disregarded altogether, but rather that the problems associated with high population should be considered within the context of a capitalist global economy.

POPULATION AND GLOBALIZATION

Overpopulation, environmental degradation, and social injustice all result from the same global economic system that seeks to increase profits at all costs. As local economies in the Third World are replaced with profit-driven, export-oriented industries – largely the result of "structural adjustment" programs imposed by the World Bank and International Monetary Fund (IMF) to benefit wealthy investors – poverty and inequality increase. This leads to higher fertility rates as poor families have more children in order to generate income and ensure economic security in their old age. As Bello points out, "inequality amidst poverty provides the most fertile conditions for high reproductive rates, just as rising living standards constitute the best guarantee that countries will experience the demographic transition to lower fertility rates."

Sri Lanka is a case in point. Since the end of World War II the Sri Lankan government sought to eliminate poverty by supporting free and subsidized food programs, higher educational levels, and greater employment opportunities for women. These limited social welfare policies have produced impressive results. Between 1960 and 1985, Sri Lanka's fertility rate dropped by a remarkable 40 percent, occurring hand-in-hand with a dramatic decline in the infant mortality rate to 27 deaths per 1,000 live births.

RAPID GROWTH

Just in the period from 1950 to 1995 – a minute in the history of people on Earth – total world population more than doubled from 2.5 billion to 5.7 billion. If fertility rates remain constant, says the UN, there will be a total of 57.2 billion people in the year 2100 and a mind-boggling 296.3 billion in 2150....

Pat M. Holt. "Population Shifts – Future Challenge Is Here." **Christian Science Monitor.** Sept. 3, 1998.

The Indian State of Kerala is another example. Like Sri Lanka, Kerala's fertility rate dropped nearly 40 percent between 1960 and 1985, and during the decades prior the government instituted a number of social welfare programs which significantly raised the living standards of the poorest sectors of society. "Fair price" shops were set up to keep the cost of rice and other essentials within reach of the poor. Increased expenditures on public health, the construction of clinics in poor areas, and land reform abolishing tenancy all greatly improved the economic security of poor families. Higher education for women also led to greater control over reproduction. As Bello reports, "the literacy rate for females in Kerala is two-and-a-half times the all-India average." All these factors contributed to Kerala's remarkable decrease in birth rates.

Even China's low birth rates were achieved during a pre-1980 system which guaranteed roughly equal access to essential goods and services. Reversing the causal connection advanced by proponents of draconian population control measures, Solon Barraclough argues: "China's one-child program would have gotten nowhere if land reform, education, health services and relative food security for the vast majority of the population had not come first." And Bello: "It was the radical opening up of access to land and food, along with an assurance of old-age security, that allowed the Chinese people to respond positively to the government's family planning program and opt for fewer children." The successes were short-lived as birth rates in China have risen since 1980 when massive economic reforms privatized agriculture and a greater part of industrial production. These privatizings have been accompanied by the erosion of many social welfare programs and

93

the widening of income inequalities. Frances Moore Lappe and Rachel Schurman explain the rise in birth rates as a direct result of these reforms: "Thrown back on their own family resources, many Chinese again see having children – especially boys – as beneficial, both as a substitute for lost public protections and as a means of taking maximum advantage of the new economic system."

SYMPTOM

Overpopulation is not so much a cause as it is a symptom of the same corporate and government policies that produce both environmental degradation and social injustice. The solutions, therefore, are not coercive population control measures like forced sterilization or militarizing the borders, but rather the radical transformation of the global economic system. On a grassroots level much of this work is already being done, but much more needs to happen....

A NATIONAL ENVIRONMENTAL POLICY: THE POINT

Lynton K. Caldwell

Lynton K. Caldwell is Professor of Public and Environmental Affairs at Indiana University. He served as Staff Consultant to the Senate Committee on the Interior and Insular Affairs on a National Policy for the Environment, 1968-1970.

■ **POINTS TO CONSIDER**

1. What is the National Environmental Policy Act (NEPA)?

2. If public opinion supports a national environmental policy, how does the author explain the public's lack of demand for implementation?

3. Describe Caldwell's policy suggestions to regain the "intent" of national environmental policy.

4. Since environmental problems are often global matters, why does the author support national environmental policy?

Excerpted from the testimony of Lynton K. Caldwell before the U.S. House Committee on Resources, March 18, 1998.

These problems of air, water, resource conservation and the biosphere were soon seen to be transnational, but national government was the only available institution sufficiently inclusive and authoritative to deal with them.

Few statutes of the United States are intrinsically more important and less understood than is the National Environmental Policy Act (NEPA) of 1969. This comprehensive legislation, the first of its kind to be adopted by any national government, and now widely emulated throughout the world, has achieved notable results, yet its basic intent has yet to be fully achieved. Its purpose and declared principles have not yet been thoroughly internalized in the assumptions and practices of American government. Nevertheless there appears to be a growing consensus among the American people that environmental quality is an enduring public value, and that development of the economy does not require a trade-off between environmental quality and economic well-being. Voluntary compliance with NEPA principles may one day become standard policy and procedure for government and business; but meanwhile it is in the interest of the Congress and the nation to understand the historical developments that led to NEPA and the subsequent course of its implementation.

UNDERSTANDING NEPA

The legislative history of NEPA and the policy concepts it declares are more extensive and accessible than some of its critics recognize. NEPA declares public values and directs policy; but it is not "regulatory" in the ordinary sense. A decade of thought, advocacy, and negotiation in and out of Congress preceded the legislation of 1969. Dissatisfaction with NEPA and its implementing institution – the Council on Environmental Quality (CEQ) – should not be directed against this innovative and well-considered statute, but rather toward failure to understand its purpose, to reinforce its administration, or to support its intent.

Through the judicially enforceable process of impact analysis, NEPA has significantly modified the environmental behavior of federal agencies, and indirectly of state and local governments and private undertakings. Relative to many other statutory policies NEPA must be accounted an important success. But implementation of the substantive principles of national policy declared in

NEPA requires a degree of political will, not yet evident in the Congress or the White House. That the American people clearly support the purpose of NEPA is evident in repeated polls of public opinion. But implementation of NEPA has not been audibly demanded by a public-at-large which has received little help in understanding what must be done to achieve objectives of which they approve.

Three decades since 1969 is a very short time for a new aspect of public policy – the environment – to attain the importance and priority accorded such century-old concerns as taxation, defense, education, civil liberties, and the economy. The goals declared in NEPA are as valid today as they were in 1969. Indeed perhaps more so as the Earth and its biosphere are stressed by human demands to a degree that has no precedent (note the 1993 World Scientists' Warning to Humanity). But "environment" in its full dimensions is not easily comprehended. Human perceptions are culturally and physically limited, but science has been extending environmental horizons from the cosmic to the microcosmic. Even so, the word "environment" does not yet carry to most people the scope, complexity, or dynamic of its true dimensions.

THE FULL INTENT

Meanwhile, for the NEPA intent to be more fully achieved two developments will be necessary:

First is greatly increased popular comprehension of the purpose and principles of environmental policy as expressed in NEPA – especially by conservation and environmental groups, civic organizations, religious denominations, and by political parties at the grass roots, along with recognition – now beginning to appear in the world of business – that economic and environmental objectives need not be incompatible. NEPA principles, if rationally applied, would help sustain the future health of both the economy and the environment.

Second is appreciation by the Congress, the executive branch, the courts, and the news media of the political responsibilities and institutional arrangements necessary to fulfill the NEPA mandate. More visible commitments in the White House and at the top policy levels of the federal agencies, and especially in the Congress are needed. As long as candidates for federal office are dependent on financing from sources whose purposes could result

in destructive exploitation of the environment, support for NEPA in the Congress and the White House is unlikely to be no more than symbolic, and seldom invoked.

NEPA, however, contains means to achieve its purpose. Institutional arrangements for coordination of policies for natural resources and, by implication, the environment, underwent extensive consultations for at least a decade preceding NEPA, within and between both houses of Congress, with the federal agencies, and with non-governmental representatives of public interests. NEPA incorporated most of the provisions upon which general agreement had been reached.

THE CASE FOR A NATIONAL POLICY

From the viewpoint of historical constitutional conservatism, environment in the broad sense was not a comprehensible subject for public policy – at least for national policy. Strict constitutional constructionist Thomas Jefferson did not even believe that highway construction was an appropriate function of the federal government. For environmental nuisances, such as air or water pollution, common law remedies were available under state police powers, and prior to the 1960s were widely regarded as local issues.

Emergence of environment as a public and national issue followed from profound changes in the population and economy of the United States in the course of the 20th century. These changes were accompanied by unprecedented growth of scientific knowledge and technology. Progress of this new industrial society increasingly encountered and created environmental problems with which neither local government or the market economy could cope. Quality of life values in health, amenities, and opportunities were being lost or threatened and the causes transcended artificial political jurisdictions.

Only the federal government had the geographic scope and institutional structure able to deal with the growing array of inter-relating problems now called "environmental." These problems of air, water, resource conservation and the biosphere were soon seen to be transnational, but national government was the only available institution sufficiently inclusive and authoritative to deal with them. International cooperation depended upon the ability and willingness of national governments to address common regional and global environmental problems and so by the mid 20th century, environment began to emerge as a new focus for public policy.

Broad statements of policy and principle that are not perceived to affect personal interests or property rights seldom arouse much public concern or response. Issues that do elicit popular concern almost always affect the present and personal advantages or apprehensions of people. Attitudes relating to the environment in modern American society have been largely issue-specific and subjective, as in the NIMBY (Not in My Back Yard) syndrome. But effective response to circumstances in the larger societal and biospheric environments necessarily must be collective, with whole communities or an organized "critical mass" of the society activated. Stratospheric ozone depletion, global climate change or tropical deforestation are hardly neighborhood or personal issues which people might feel that their actions could influence. And while non-governmental organizations may help in many ways to assist environmental protection, the ultimate agent of public interests affecting all of the United States is the federal government. State and county boundaries are environmentally artificial, corresponding neither to ecosystems nor bioregions, and seldom to economic activities that are increasingly interstate, nationwide, and trans-national in scope.

CONCLUSION

NEPA is potentially a powerful statute, well integrated, internally consistent, and flexible, even though not entirely clear on some points of law which have nevertheless been clarified by interpretation, as in the Regulations issued by the CEQ under Executive Order 11991 of 1977. That it has made a significant difference in the United States and has influenced governments abroad is hardly debatable. NEPA was not a sudden inspiration, nor was it put over on an unsuspecting Congress and the public by an environmental lobby. Its purpose was never the writing of impact statements; but this action-forcing procedure has been a great inducement to ecological rationality in federal actions which traditionally had largely ignored environmental consequences.

A NATIONAL ENVIRONMENTAL POLICY: THE COUNTERPOINT

Lynn Scarlett

Lynn Scarlett is Director of the Reason Public Policy Institute and Vice President for Research at the Reason Foundation. She is the author of numerous articles on environmental policy, privatization and local economic development. Since 1993, Scarlett has served as chair of the "How Clean Is Clean" Working Group of the Washington, D.C.-based National Environmental Policy Institute.

■ **POINTS TO CONSIDER**

1. Why was the U.S. national environment policy unique, according to the author?

2. Discuss the impact of citizens in the environmental review process.

3. Identify at least two flaws in the national environmental policy of the U.S. in the author's view.

4. Evaluate Scarlett's suggestions for policy reform.

Excerpted from the testimony of Lynn Scarlett before the U.S. House Committee on Resources, March 18, 1998.

Critics of delays view the National Environmental Policy Act (NEPA) as having moved away from its vision of balance to one in which a particular set of environmental values has eclipsed other values or concerns.

At its inception three decades ago, the National Environmental Policy Act (NEPA) was in several ways unique. First, unlike other environmental laws passed in the years that followed, NEPA explicitly set forth a goal of balancing environmental values with other social and economic values, using language such as "productive harmony" between "man and nature" and emphasizing the importance of environmental, social, and economic requirements. Second, unlike other environmental statutes, NEPA took a "big picture" approach, requiring that agencies examine the web of environmental impacts that might be associated with federal projects and activities rather than focusing on single-medium impacts. Third, NEPA was not prescriptive: it attempted to establish procedures through which environmental values could be more systematically considered by federal agencies in project planning and decisions. Balance, a holistic perspective, and the prospect of flexible responses all characterized NEPA in concept.

BREAKING PROMISES

In practice, NEPA has not always fulfilled its promise, having unleashed some unintended consequences and procedural inefficiencies.

On the one hand, some of its critics note its use by some citizen groups as a tool to delay and stop projects altogether rather than to improve them and mitigate environmental harms. Use of NEPA in this way has not been uniform across all federal projects but, instead, has been more evident in a few particularly contentious areas such as highway projects, mining projects, and forest management. Highway projects, for example, often take from two to eight years to complete the NEPA and related permitting processes. Critics of these delays view NEPA as having moved away from its vision of balance to one in which a particular set of environmental values has eclipsed other values or concerns.

On the other hand, many agencies have only reluctantly engaged in the NEPA process, seeing it as one more law with which they must comply, but not viewing NEPA as an integral part of their planning and decision making process. The result of this compliance attitude has been a failure to take seriously the information that emerges through preparation of environmental impact statements (EIS). Project choices are essentially decided before the EIS process has been completed, and EIS results then fail to result in project modifications. Equally important, once the project is under way, little or no ongoing monitoring and evaluation of environmental impacts occurs that, if done, might allow for ongoing mitigations, adjustments, or improvements.

CITIZEN EXPERIENCE

This failure is especially important to the focus of today: citizen experience. Citizens who participate in the EIS review process often have an opportunity to comment only after a project alternative has been selected. Their participation is, thus, minimal in any meaningful sense.

There is a third problem with NEPA as practiced: the review process can be time-consuming and costly – sometimes without any clear benefits emerging as a consequence of the time and effort spent. Within the Department of Energy (DOE), for example, until recent changes were enacted, the median time for completing an EIS was nearly three years. But the median figure understates the problem. For individual projects, the EIS process sometimes has taken six or more years.

Documents have often included hundreds of pages, often in arcane and technical jargon inaccessible to the general public. One study of the typical language used in environmental impact reports concluded that the reports were geared to a reader with a college degree or higher.

REINVENTION PROGRESS AND LIMITS

None of these criticisms of the NEPA process is new. Over the last decade the Council on Environmental Quality (CEQ) and various federal agencies have been acutely aware of the cumbersome, costly, inefficient, and time-consuming nature of the NEPA process. Self-criticism has abounded. In its most recent assessment of NEPA, the CEQ underscored problems of timeliness, lack of coordination among multiple agencies involved in a single project, lack of robust public participation, and lack of ongoing evaluation or monitoring.

This self-reflection has yielded numerous attempts at reinvention, both spearheaded by CEQ and undertaken by individual agencies. Notable among these efforts has been the deliberate attempt by the Department of Energy to streamline its NEPA processes. Specifically, the DOE has carefully evaluated the circumstances under which an EIS is appropriate and has delineated specific areas for "categorical exclusion" to avoid lengthy evaluations where impacts can be expected to be minimal. Equally important, the DOE set specific goals for reducing the median timeline to 15 months and tracks both costs and timelines for all environmental assessments (EAs) and EISs. Moreover, the cost and time information is published and available to the public in easily accessible form.

This effort by the DOE has some positive results. The common wisdom that "what gets measured gets done" is accurate in the case of the DOE. By setting specific timeline goals, and publishing performance in meeting those goals, agency decision makers have a stronger incentive to move the NEPA process forward in order to meet the agency's stated goals. Since implementing its reinvention procedures, DOE's record has improved – median completion times have dropped from nearly three years to under twenty months.

OPTION AND STATUTORY CONSIDERATIONS

As many as seventy federal agencies are subject to NEPA process requirements. In any given project, sometimes as many as thirty public agencies from federal, state, local, and tribal governments may be involved in the review process. The number of potential participants in the NEPA process for any given project opens up substantial prospect for conflict and delays.

While some of these agencies have succeeded in coordinating the timing of the EIS process with other project permit processes, and some have succeeded in coordinating their input early on in the review scoping, these efforts are not required, and there are no mechanisms to enforce coordination and cooperation. Nor are there systematic means of resolving disputes. It is not clear that altering CEQ guidelines or other administrative efforts can accomplish consistent coordination and conflict resolution.

Second, the existing NEPA statute does not establish clear requirements for public participation during the up-front or scoping process. Nor are clear limits set regarding the nature and timing of public input – with the result that uncertainty and time delays with late public input sometimes occur.

Third, current law has no clear requirements for agencies to report either costs or length of time to complete EAs and EISs on an average and/or median basis. Elsewhere among several states, time-reporting requirements for other permitting processes have resulted in substantial improvements in expediting permit processes. NEPA has no parallel requirements, though individual agencies like the DOE do engage in such reporting.

Fourth, substantial ongoing disputes and conflict continue over scoping and focus of NEPA reviews. While individual agencies have developed categorical exclusions, greater clarity on "what counts" and "what doesn't" may reduce litigation and delays.

MEDIATION, DISCLOSURE

Congress may wish to consider establishing requirements for negotiation, mediation, and conflict resolution. Currently, alternative dispute resolution (ADR) tools are available to CEQ and agencies involved in NEPA reviews. However, use of such tools is sporadic and serendipitous. Moreover, there is no mechanism to require participation in conflict resolution. An ADR process might not only establish procedures for early public input into scoping and other NEPA steps, but also set forth procedures for determining a proposed participant's standing in a particular matter.

A second option Congress may wish to consider is that of cost and timing information disclosure. Such disclosure is currently permissible but not required. Several states have begun to experiment with such disclosure in other environmental permitting processes. The State of Oklahoma, for example, publishes permit status and the length of time permit applications have been under review for various environmental permits. The information also names the particular lead officer charged with processing a particular permit. The result of this mere publication of permit times has resulted in substantial reductions in permit delays. While not perfectly applicable to the NEPA circumstance, the concept of disclosure of such information may create some incentive by project decision makers to expedite proceedings and limit review to essential issues, helping to counter the incentive some now have to "over-evaluate."

DIRTY WATER

Water quality is another serious environmental problem. Half of the world's population is estimated to suffer from infections caused by waterborne diseases such as yellow fever, malaria and river blindness. Diseases associated with water kill five million people per year, and four of five child deaths in developing countries result from waterborne disease....

Terry Anderson and Donald R. Wentworth. "Water, Water Everywhere, But Can We Drink It?" **Social Education.** Oct. 1997: 337-9.

LIMITS OF CHANGE

No change of NEPA can entirely resolve some of the problems its procedures invoke. And no change of NEPA will result in all of the hoped-for environmental benefits that its architects and current champions envision. There is one fundamental reason for these limitations.

Some agencies, by their mission and current structure, face internal agency incentives that work against integrating economic and environmental protection goals. For example, funding arrangements of the Forest Service discourage forest managers from undertaking some conservation measures and encourage them to promote other uneconomic and environmentally damaging practices. NEPA processes can identify the impacts of certain proposed projects but cannot change the internal incentives faced by the agency and which drive decisions. This incentive problem is well-documented in much public-choice literature on park service management, forestry management, and so on.

Improving NEPA both to streamline it and to build it more into a problem-solving rather than compliance-focused process may help "harmonize" economic, social, and environmental values, as the original statute set out to accomplish, and may yield some environmental and efficiency improvements. But some of these improvements will be limited unless parallel changes in incentive structures within individual agencies are also undertaken.

INTERPRETING EDITORIAL CARTOONS

This activity may be used as an individualized study guide for students in libraries and resource centers or as a discussion catalyst in small group and classroom discussions.

Although cartoons are usually humorous, the main intent of most political cartoonists is not to entertain. Cartoons express serious social comment about important issues. Using graphics and visual arts, the cartoonist expresses opinions and attitudes. By employing an entertaining and often light-hearted visual format, cartoonists may have as much or more impact on national and world issues as editorial and syndicated columnists.

Points to Consider:

1. Examine the cartoon in Reading Twelve.

2. How would you describe the message of the cartoon? Try to describe the message in one to three sentences.

3. Do you agree with the message expressed in the cartoon? Why or why not?

4. Does the cartoon support the author's point of view in any of the readings in this book? If the answer is yes, be specific about which reading or readings and why.

5. Are any readings in Chapter Two in basic agreement with this cartoon?

CHAPTER 3

ENVIRONMENT, ECONOMY, AND ETHICS: IDEAS IN CONFLICT

SHIFTING PARADIGMS: FOCUS ON PROPERTY RIGHTS

Roy E. Cordato

Roy E. Cordato is the Lundy Professor at Campbell University in Buies Creek, North Carolina. The following article appeared in The Freeman, *a monthly publication of the Foundation for Economic Education, Inc. (FEE). FEE is a nonprofit education organization which promotes private property, limited government and the free market.*

■ POINTS TO CONSIDER

1. Explain the standard view of the cause of environmental problems, according to Cordato.

2. Identify the cause of environmental problems in the author's view. Is this a failure of government or market?

3. Describe the property rights approach to environmental problems. What do you think of this perspective?

4. Contrast free market environmentalism with market-based environmentalism (MBE).

5. According to the article, what are the two most common MBE approaches? Summarize the author's critique of the two.

Excerpted from Cordato, Roy E. "Market-Based Environmentalism vs. the Free Market." **The Freeman.** Sept. 1997: 555-7. © 1997 The Foundation for Economic Education, Inc.

Environmental problems occur because property rights, a prerequisite of free markets, are not identified or enforced.

The standard view of environmental problems is that they are inherent in a free society. If people are left free to pursue their own self-interest – to produce and consume whatever they want, how and when they want it – the result will be polluted air and waterways, littered streets, and depleted natural resources. Pollution and environmental degradation are often cited as evidence that Adam Smith was wrong. People pursuing their own self-interest may not advance the well-being of society.

MARKET-BASED ENVIRONMENTALISM (MBE)

Advocates of MBE fully subscribe to this view. As MBE advocates Robert Stavins and Bradley Whitehead argue, "policies are needed to...harness the power of market forces...to link the...forces of government and industry."

That view, unfortunately found in many economic texts, misunderstands the nature of both a free society and a free-market economy. Environmental problems occur because property rights, a prerequisite of free markets, are not identified or enforced. Problems of air, river, and ocean pollution are all due to a lack of private property rights or protection. Since clarifying and enforcing property rights is the basic function of government in a free society, environmental problems are an example of government failure, not market failure.

In a free society, environmental problems should be viewed in terms of how they impinge on human liberty. Questions should focus on how and why one person's use of resources might interfere with the planning and the decision-making abilities of others. Since people can legitimately make plans and decisions only with respect to resources that they have rights to, environmentalism that has human well-being as the focus of its analysis must center on property rights.

CLEAR PROPERTY RIGHTS

From this perspective, environmental problems arise because different people attempt to use the same resource for conflicting purposes. This can occur only if the property rights to that resource are not clear or are not being enforced. Two simple examples can highlight the possibilities. Imagine a community that has a cement factory that emits cement dust into the air. The dust causes people in the community to have to wash their cars and house windows more frequently than otherwise and creates respiratory problems for those who have to breathe it. That is clearly a property-rights enforcement problem. Note that the problem is not that the dust is emitted into the air but that it lands on people's property – their cars, houses, and lungs – and interferes with their use of it. In this case, ownership rights are clearly defined, but are not enforced.

Another example might involve a public waterway, such as a river. Along the river, there is a factory that dumps the waste from its production process. Downstream are homeowners who use the river for recreational purposes, possibly fishing or swimming. The factory waste renders the river unsuitable or less useful for those purposes. The central problem here is that the rights to the river are not clearly defined. The public-policy issue involves who should have those rights or how they should be divided. It should be noted that the idea of privatizing rivers or sections of rivers is not new. Early American Indian tribes had clearly defined and enforced property rights to sections of many rivers. State governments nullified those rights.

Since free markets require well-defined and enforced property rights, the solution to environmental problems lies in extending capitalism, not restricting it.

ALTERING INCENTIVES

Market-based environmentalism has little in common with this approach. Under MBE, government authorities deem a level of effluent emissions, the amount of recycled paper in grocery bags, or some other outcome a desirable goal. Individual behavior is then manipulated to achieve the goal. MBE policies are meant to control markets by altering the incentive structure – that is, individual decision-making – in order to thwart the outcomes of free-market activity.

Even the free-market advocate and chairman of President Reagan's Council of Economic Advisers, Murray Weidenbaum, has argued, "The environmental pollution problem is not the negative task of punishing wrongdoers. Rather, the challenge is a very positive one: to alter people's incentives."

The two most common MBE approaches are excise taxes and "tradable permits." The excise tax is a direct implication of traditional welfare economics, which argues that pollution is evidence of "market failure" in which prices fail to incorporate the full "social cost" of production; that is, the external costs associated with the pollution are left out. Since, under this theory, markets fail to generate the correct price and output, an excise tax equivalent to the pollution costs would "correct" for the failure. The problem is that this entire analysis is both practically and conceptually unworkable. The concept of social cost, if meaningful at all, would be the sum of the pollution costs experienced by all the individuals in the community. Yet in reality, each person's costs are strictly personal and subjectively experienced. They cannot be measured and certainly cannot be added to the "pollution costs" experienced by others.

UNWORKABILITY

Furthermore, because any tax would cause a complete reallocation of resources in the economy, it could not possibly be known whether the tax would end up making society as a whole better or worse off. Such policies ignore not only sound economics but also sound science. The result is proposals that promote the political agenda or aesthetic values of policymakers and interest groups.

For example, the World Resources Institute (WRI) has published a study claiming that the use of automobiles imposes $300 billion annually in external costs on society. That figure includes the "costs" of global warming, even though decades of satellite data actually show mostly global cooling, and such pure aesthetics as the unsightliness of shopping malls and the loss of open space due to urban sprawl. The proposed remedies are all "market-based" and meant to "alter people's incentives." They include hefty new taxes on gasoline, user fees for roads, and forcing all shopping malls to charge for parking.

Tradable permits (TPs), while often referred to as a "property rights" approach, are not intended to expand property rights but to rearrange and restrict existing ones to achieve an "environmentally correct" and politically determined result. This approach begins by identifying an undesirable activity and then restricting it by issuing a fixed number of permits to pursue the activity. The permits then can be bought and sold in a market setting. Firms can boost their revenues by reducing the level of the activity in question and selling permits to other firms that wish to increase their activity beyond what their permits allow. While TPs "harness" market forces to achieve politically determined environmental goals, they are in fact disdainful of truly free markets based on the recognition and enforcement of property rights.

LEGAL VIOLATIONS

TPs simply legalize trespass to the extent they allow actual rights-violating pollution to continue, for example, allowing cement companies in the example above to pollute without compensation to victims. As Robert McGee and Walter Block have argued, "perhaps the major fault with trading permits is that ...they entail a fundamental and pervasive violation of property rights."

In other instances, they simply create new kinds of rights in an attempt to centrally plan industries in the name of environmental protection. The Progressive Policy Institute, President Clinton's favorite think tank, is calling for tradable permits to promote recycling. The government would issue permits to newsprint companies limiting them to a certain level of nonrecycled materials in their paper. Companies could sell their permits if they increase the recycled content. Those proposals exist, even though, as reported in the *Washington Post* and the *Wall Street Journal,* too much recycling may be causing increased pollution and waste of resources. Such policies are best viewed as an attempt to impose personal attitudes, such as a disdain for landfills, on society.

HUMAN FOCUS

Market-based environmentalism and the free market are not the same. Free-market policies, even with respect to the environment, would not have "environmental protection" *per se* as their central focus. Instead the focus would be on resolving conflicts among human beings as they put natural resources to use. An important by-product of that would be a cleaner environment and a more conscientious stewardship of resources.

MBE sees human activity as something that must be harnessed by the government, albeit through market incentives. The conflict, from this perspective, is not among human beings but between them and the natural environment, with human beings wearing the black hats.

SHIFTING PARADIGMS: SUSTAINABILITY IS THE ANSWER

James M. Wall

James M. Wall is the editor of The Christian Century. The Christian Century *is an ecumenical weekly journal of current events, politics, and culture.*

■ POINTS TO CONSIDER

1. How does the author distinguish between "economic development" and "sustainability?"

2. What does "conversion" signify in this reading?

3. Summarize "a typical day on the planet" in Orr and Wall's view.

4. Identify reasons for religious communities' lack of awareness with regard to environmental issues.

Wall, James M. "In Jeopardy." **The Christian Century.** December 3, 1997: 1115-6. © 1997 Christian Century Foundation. Reprinted by permission from the December 3, 1997 issue of **The Christian Century.**

...we are living on borrowed time on this planet, which is being overheated by global warming and seriously depleted by our focus on economic development rather than sustainability.

A gentle rain falls on a high bluff overlooking the Pacific Ocean. Below, huge waves crash against the beach and then recede. The sight of that vast ocean evokes a sense of the majesty of creation. But what is even more important to me in this moment is the sound of the rain, a gentle reminder of rains of the past, soothing in its regularity and reassuring as a sign that another Southern California rainy season has begun. Soon I drive along a crowded freeway. Ordinarily I would be concentrating so tensely on the road that I would hardly notice either the ocean or the rain, but now I am touched by a sense of calm. It is related, I begin to realize, to the sound of the rain. Perhaps, having just spent three days among people who care passionately for the earth, I've had a conversion.

EARTH IN DANGER

This network of scholars is warning us that the earth is in danger. As Oberlin College Professor David Orr puts it, "Many things on which our future health and prosperity depend are in dire jeopardy: climate stability, the resilience and productivity of natural systems, the beauty of the natural world, and biological diversity." Theologian John Cobb stresses that we are living on borrowed time on this planet, which is being overheated by global warming and seriously depleted by our focus on economic development rather than sustainability.

Cobb suggested I sit in on a conference on "pedagogy in a just and sustainable world" that met at Claremont School of Theology. It was also Cobb who started me thinking about conversion. He has written of his own conversion experience: "In the summer of 1969, my son Cliff helped open my eyes to what human beings are doing to our shared natural environment. For the first time I saw the meaning of the finitude of the world and began to understand the pressure of human activity upon its capacities... I saw that the ways I had previously envisaged that human problems were to be progressively alleviated would not work, that they only hastened catastrophe" *(Sustaining the Common Good).*

AWAY FROM "ECONOMISM"

Talk of conversion comes naturally to Cobb, a product of Georgia Methodism who at the University of Chicago latched on to process philosophy as a way of interpreting classic Christian doctrine in the context of scientific modernism. Now retired from Claremont School of Theology, Cobb devotes his energies to the struggle to reorient modern thought away from "economism" – his term for an exclusive focus on the gross national product – toward a concern for the earth, which some environmental activists refer to as the "body of God."

Our culture continues to have only passing interest in sustainable development. One writer has noted that we start our children down the path toward exploiting nature rather than caring for it when we confine them to classrooms for their schooling and release them only briefly to go outside and play – on asphalt. This leaves little room for an awareness or appreciation of the natural world. The conference at Claremont focused on how teachers from kindergarten to graduate school can offset this bias against the environment.

DISTURBING FACTS

After listening to these folks for three days, I realized that, like Paul's hearers at the Areopagus, I was already committed to the redemptive world they were preaching but have my own terms for it: I call it an awareness of mystery and a reverence for life. What I learned at the conference was the magnitude of the problem and the urgent need to reshape our thinking. Orr's essay "What Is Education?" spells out the disturbing facts:

"If today is a typical day on planet earth, we will lose 116 square miles of rain forest, or about an acre a second. We will lose another 72 miles to encroaching deserts, the results of human mismanagement and overpopulation. We will lose 40 to 250 species, and no one knows whether the number is 40 or 250. Today the human population will increase by 250,000. And today we will add 2,700 tons of chlorofluorocarbons and 15 million tons of carbon dioxide to the atmosphere. Tonight the earth will be a little hotter, its waters more acidic, and the fabric of life more threadbare. By the year's end the numbers are staggering: The total loss of rain forest will equal an area the size of the state of Washington; expanding deserts will equal an area the size of the

state of West Virginia; and the global population will have risen by more than 90,000,000. By the year 2000 perhaps as much as 20 percent of the life forms extant on the planet in the year 1900 will be extinct."

UNBRIDLED GROWTH

Religious communities have been slow to acknowledge the threat imposed by unbridled economic growth. Much of the awareness that has arisen can be traced to the environmental emphasis of the World Council of Churches (WCC). In *Sustaining the Common Good* Cobb writes that the WCC has long pressed for "a just and participatory society rather than economic growth." But "as awareness of the ecological crisis dawned, there was growing realization that something was missing from the formulation." The word "sustainable" was added at the WCC's Nairobi Assembly in 1975, committing the WCC to a goal of a "just, participatory and sustainable society."

That goal received some strong theological support recently from Ecumenical Patriarch Bartholomew, spiritual leader of the world's Orthodox Christians, who spoke on the threat to the planet at a symposium at Santa Barbara. Bartholomew, who was formerly on the staff of the WCC, has been called the "green patriarch" because of his strong support for earth issues. Pointing specifically to human-caused deforestation, species extinction, wetland destruction and toxic pollution, Bartholomew declared, "To commit a crime against the natural world is a sin." When we lose species, land and creatures, we lose a part of God's creative process, not through natural selection but by deliberate destruction on the part of an economic system driven by the god of profit.

TRUTH DISAPPEARS

In *Another Country,* Christopher Camuto addresses this destruction with this lament: "True places, and with them part of the truth, disappear daily. The much-descried destruction of nature – especially the logging of forests, the damming of rivers, the pollution of air and water, and the overdevelopment of rural landscapes – leads, among other disadvantages, to the erasure of history. You only have to approach the Great Smoky Mountains from Sevierville, Tennessee, Pigeon Forge and Gatlinburg, perhaps the ugliest stretch of road in eastern North America, to see the deep past and immediate future juxtaposed in a very confused present moment, a weird snarl of traffic and herd consumerism foregrounding one of the most magnificent landscapes on earth."

Bartholomew is right: we are guilty of the sin of breaking our relationship with God when we allow herd consumerism to destroy both the truth of our history and the healing beauty of God's creation.

READING

19

A DOOMSAYER'S VIEW: GLOBAL RESOURCES ARE UNDERVALUED

Janet N. Abramovitz

Janet N. Abramovitz is a senior researcher at the Worldwatch Institute. Worldwatch Institute is a nonprofit public policy research organization which informs the public about emerging global problems and trends – focusing upon the world economy and its effect upon environmental support systems. Contact Worldwatch at 1776 Massachusetts Avenue, NW, Washington, D.C. 20036-1904, www.worldwatch.org/.

■ **POINTS TO CONSIDER**

1. According to Abramovitz, what is happening to natural ecosystems? What are the costs of damaging ecosystems?

2. Describe the measures currently used to value natural resources.

3. Define the phrase "socializing costs."

4. What role does consumption play in changing current valuations of ecosystems?

Excerpted from Abramovitz, Janet N. "Putting a Value on Nature's 'Free' Services." **Worldwatch.** Jan./Feb. 1998: 10-9. Reprinted with permission, Worldwatch Institute.

With a zero value, it's easy to see why nature has almost always been the loser in standard economic equations.

Around the world, the degradation, fragmentation, and simplification – or "conversion" – of ecosystems is progressing rapidly. Today, only one to five percent of the original forest cover of the United States and Europe remains. One-third of Asia's forest has been lost since 1960, and half of what remains is threatened by the same industrial forest activities responsible for the Indonesian fires. In the Amazon, 13 percent of the natural cover has already been cleared, mostly for cattle pasture. In many countries, including some of the largest, more than half of the land has been converted from natural habitat to other uses that are less resilient. In countries that stayed relatively undisturbed until the 1980s, significant portions of remaining ecosystems have been lost in the last decade. These trends have been accelerating everywhere. As the natural ecosystems disappear, so do many of the goods and services they provide.

SINGLE COMMODITY PRODUCTION

That may seem to contradict the premise that people want those goods and services and would not deliberately destroy them. But there's a logical explanation: governments and business owners typically perceive that the way they can make the most profit from an ecosystem is to maximize its production of a single commodity, such as timber from a forest. For the community (or society) as a whole, however, that is often the least profitable or sustainable use. The economic values of other uses, and the number of people who benefit, added up, can be enormous. A forest, if not cut down to make space for a one-commodity plantation, can produce a rich variety of non-timber forest products on one hand, while providing essential watershed protection and climate regulation, on the other. These uses not only have more immediate economic value but can also be sustained over a longer term and benefit more people....

THE OTHER SERVICE ECONOMY

Natural services have been so undervalued because, for so long, we have viewed the natural world as an inexhaustible resource and sink. Human impact has been seen as insignificant or beneficial. The tools used to gauge the economic health and progress of a nation have tended to reinforce and encourage these attitudes. The gross domestic product (GDP), for example, supposedly measures the value of the goods and services produced in a nation. But the most valuable goods and services – the ones provided by nature, on which all else rests – are measured poorly or not at all. The unhealthy dynamic is compounded by the fact that activities that pollute or deplete natural capital are counted as contributions to economic wellbeing. As ecologist Norman Myers puts it, "Our tools of economic analysis are far from able to apprehend, let alone comprehend, the entire range of values implicit in forests."

When economies and societies use misleading signals about what is valuable, people are encouraged to make decisions that run counter to their own long-range interests – and those of society and future generations. Economic calculations grossly underestimate the current and future value of nature. While a fraction of nature's goods are counted when they enter the marketplace, many of them are not. And nature's services – the life-support systems – are not counted at all. When the goods are considered free and therefore valued at zero, the market sends signals that they are only economically valuable when converted into something else. For example, the profit from deforesting land is counted as a plus on a nation's ledger sheet, because the trees have been converted to saleable lumber or pulp, but the depletions of the timber stock, watershed, and fisheries are not subtracted.

VALUE OF ECOSYSTEMS

In 1997, an international team of researchers led by Robert Costanza of the University of Maryland's Institute for Ecological Economics, published a landmark study on the importance of nature's services in supporting human economies. The study provides, for the first time, a quantification of the current economic value of the world's ecosystem services and natural capital. The researchers synthesized the findings of over 100 studies to compute the average per hectare value for each of the 17 services that world's ecosystems provide. They concluded that the current economic value of the world's ecosystem services is in the neighborhood of $33 trillion per year, exceeding the global aggregate of gross national product (GNP) of $25 trillion.

Placing a monetary value on nature in this way has been criticized by those who believe that it commoditizes and cheapens nature's infinite value. But in practice, we all regularly assign value to nature through the choices we make. The problem is that in normal practice, many of us don't assign such value to nature until it is converted to something man-made – forests to timber, or swimming fish to a restaurant meal. With a zero value, it's easy to see why nature has almost always been the loser in standard economic equations. As the authors of the Costanza study note, "...the decisions we make about ecosystems imply valuations (although not necessarily expressed in monetary terms). We can choose to make these valuations explicit or not...but as long as we are forced to make choices, we are going through the process of valuation." The study is also raising a powerful new challenge to those traditional economists who are accustomed to keeping environmental costs and benefits "external" to their calculations.

While some skeptics will doubtless argue that the global valuation reported by Costanza and his colleagues overestimates the current value of nature's services, if anything it is actually a very conservative estimate. As the authors point out, values for some biomes (such as mountains, arctic tundra, deserts, urban parks) were not included. Further, they note that as ecosystem services become scarcer, their economic value will only increase.

SOCIALIZING COSTS

Clearly, failure to value nature's services is not the only reason why these services are misused. Too often, illogical and inequitable resource use continues – even in the face of evidence that it is ecologically, economically, and socially unsustainable – because powerful interests are able to shape policies by legal or illegal means. Frequently, some individuals or entities get the financial benefits from a resource while the losses are distributed across society. Economists call this "socializing costs." Stated simply, the people who get the benefits are not the ones who pay the costs. Thus, there is little economic incentive for those exploiting a resource to use it judiciously or in a manner that maximizes public good. Where laws are lax or are ignored, and where people do not have an opportunity for meaningful participation in decision-making, such abuses will continue.

The liquidation of 90 percent of the Philippines' forest during the 1970s and 1980s under the Ferdinand Marcos dictatorship, for example, made a few hundred families over $42 billion richer. But 18 million forest dwellers became much poorer. The nation as a whole went from being the world's second largest log exporter to a net importer. Likewise, in Indonesia today, the "benefits" from burning the forest will enrich a relatively few well-connected individuals and companies but tens of millions of others are bearing the costs. Even in wealthy nations, such as Canada, the forest industry wields heavy influence over how the forests are managed, and for whose benefit.

UNPREDICTABLE CONSEQUENCES

We have already seen that the loss of ecosystem services can have severe economic, social, and ecological costs even though we can only measure a fraction of them. The loss of timber and lives in the Indonesian fires, and the lower production of fruits and vegetables from inadequate pollination, are but the tip of the iceberg. The other consequences for nature are often unforeseen and unpredictable. The loss of individual species and habitat, and the degradation and simplification of ecosystems, impair nature's ability to provide the services we need. Many of these changes are irreversible, and much of what is lost is simply irreplaceable.

By reducing the number of species and the size and integrity of ecosystems, we are also reducing nature's capacity to evolve and create new life. Almost half of the forests that once covered the Earth are now gone, and much of what remains is in fragmented patches. In just a few centuries we have gone from living off nature's interest to spending down the capital that has accumulated over millions of years of evolution. At the same time we are diminishing the capacity of nature to create new capital. Humans are only one part of the evolutionary product. Yet we have taken on a major role in shaping its future production course and potential. We are pulling out the threads of nature's safety net even as we depend on it to support the world's expanding human population and economy.

CHANGING CONSUMPTION HABITS

In that expanding economy, consumers now need to recognize that it is possible to reduce and reverse the destructive impact of our activities by consuming less and by placing fewer demands on those services we have so mistakenly regarded as free. We can, for example, reduce the high levels of waste and over-consumption of timber and paper. We can also increase the efficiency of water and energy use. In agricultural fields we can leave hedgerows and unplowed areas that serve as nesting and feeding sites for pollinators. We can sharply reduce reliance on agricultural chemicals, and improve the timing of their application to avoid killing pollinators.

Maintaining nature's services requires looking beyond the needs of the present generation, with the goal of ensuring sustainability for many generations to come. We have no honest choice but to act under the assumption that future generations will need at least the same level of nature's services as we have today. We can neither practically nor ethically decide what future generations will need and what they can survive without.

A CORNUCOPIAN VIEW: GLOBAL DEGRADATION IS IMAGINED

Julian Simon

The late Julian Simon, Ph.D., was a Professor of business administration at the University of Maryland. An adjunct scholar at the Cato Institute, Simon studied the economics of population for more than 25 years.

■ POINTS TO CONSIDER

1. Who is Paul Ehrlich?

2. Describe the discourse surrounding the environment circa 1970.

3. According to Simon, what are the facts about the state of humanity and the environment?

4. Describe the contemporary scientific consensus.

Simon, Julian. "Why Do Environmentalists Persist in Imagining Global Degradation?" **Human Events.** May 5, 1995: 11. Reprinted with permission.

...astonishing as it may seem, there are no data showing that conditions are deteriorating. Rather, all indicators show that the quality of human life has been getting better.

April 22, 1995, marked the 25th anniversary of Earth Day. Now as then its message was spiritually uplifting. But all reasonable persons who look at the latest statistical evidence must agree that Earth Day's scientific premises are entirely wrong.

During the first great Earth Week in 1970 there was panic. The doomsaying environmentalists – of whom the dominant figure was Paul Ehrlich – had raised the alarm: The oceans and the Great Lakes were dying; impending great famines would be seen on television starting in 1975; the death rate would quickly increase due to pollution, and rising prices of increasingly scarce raw materials would lead to a reversal in the past centuries' progress in the standard of living.

The media trumpeted the bad news in headlines and front-page stories. Ehrlich was on the Johnny Carson show for an unprecedented full hour – twice. Classes were given by television to tens of thousands of university students.

It is hard for those who did not experience it to imagine the national excitement then. Even those who never read a newspaper joined in efforts to clean up streams, and the most repentant slobs refrained from littering for a few weeks.

OVERPOPULATION SCARE

Population growth was the great bugaboo. Every ill was the result of too many people in the United States and abroad. The remedy, doomsayers urged, was government-coerced birth control, abroad and even at home.

On the evening before Earth Day, I spoke on a panel at the jam-packed auditorium at the University of Illinois. The organizers had invited me to provide "balance." I spoke then exactly the same ideas that I write today; some of the very words are the same.

Of the 2,000 persons in attendance, probably fewer than a dozen concluded that anything I said made sense. A panelist denounced me as a religious nut, attributing to me weird beliefs,

Cartoon by Andrew Singer. Reprinted with permission.

such as that murder was the equivalent of celibacy. My ten-minute talk so enraged people that it led to a physical brawl with another professor.

Every statement I made in 1970 about the trends in resource scarcity and environmental cleanliness turned out to be correct. Every prediction has been validated by events. Yet the World Bank, the United Nations Fund for Population Activities, the U.S. Agency for International Development, the CIA, and the Clinton Administration still take as doctrine exactly the same ideas expressed by the doomsayers in 1970.

Here are the facts: On average, people throughout the world have been living longer and eating better than ever before. Fewer people die from famine nowadays than in earlier centuries. The real prices of food and of every other raw material are lower now than in earlier decades and centuries, indicating a trend of increased natural resource availability rather than increased scarcity. Major air and water pollutants in the advanced countries have been lessening rather than worsening.

In short, every single measure of material and environmental welfare in the United States has improved rather than deteriorated. This is also true of the world taken as a whole. All the long-run trends point in exactly the opposite direction from the projections of the doomsayers.

There have been, and always will be, temporary and local exceptions to these broad trends. But astonishing as it may seem, there are no data showing that conditions are deteriorating. Rather, all indicators show that the quality of human life has been getting better.

SHIFT AMONG SCIENTISTS

As a result of this evidence of improvement rather than degradation, in the past few years there has been a major shift in scientific opinion away from the views the doomsayers espouse. There now are dozens of books in print and hundreds of articles in the technical and popular literature reporting these facts.

Responding to the accumulating literature that shows no negative correlation between population growth and economic development, in 1986 the National Academy of Scientists (NAS) published a report on population growth and economic development prepared by a prestigious scholarly group. It reversed almost completely the frightening conclusions of the previous 1971 NAS report.

The group found no quantitative statistical evidence of population growth's hindering economic progress, though they hedged their qualitative judgment a bit. The report found benefits of additional people as well as costs. Even the World Bank, the greatest institutional worrier about population growth, reported in 1984 that the world's natural resource situation provides no reason to limit population growth.

A bet between Ehrlich and me epitomizes the matter. In 1980, ten years after the first Earth Day, Ehrlich and two associates wagered with me about future prices of raw materials. We would assess the trend in $1,000 worth of copper, chrome, nickel, tin and tungsten for ten years. I would win if resources grew more abundant and thus cheaper and they would win if resources became scarcer and thus more expensive. At settling time in 1990, the year of the 20th Earth Week, they sent me a check for $576.07.

A single bet proves little, of course. Hence I have offered to

PEOPLE ARE A GOOD THING

Julian Simon and many environmentalists differed in their evaluation of markets and technology. (Simon liked both, a lot.) But the greatest difference is in the two sides' views of human beings. For environmentalists, there are too many of us and we consume too much. It is only a slight exaggeration to say that many environmentalists view humans like the yeast used to brew beer: mindlessly and uncontrollably we reproduce and reproduce until finally we will suffocate in our own waste. Simon's view of people can be expressed simply: the more, the merrier. Individuals are the source of innovation, imagination, and creativity. This is why markets work and technology is a good thing. Humans are, to use the title of Simon's most important book, "the ultimate resource...."

John Clark. "Simon Says: 'Lighten Up and Look at the Facts.'" **American Outlook.** Spring 1998: 56.

repeat the wager and I have broadened it as follows: I'll bet a week's or a month's pay that any trend pertaining to material human welfare will improve rather than get worse. You pick the trend – perhaps life expectancy, the price of a natural resource, some measure of air or water pollution or the number of telephones per person – and you choose the area of the world and the future year the comparison is to be made. If I win, my winnings go to nonprofit research.

I have not been able to close another deal with a prominent academic doomsayer. They all continue to warn of impending deterioration, but they refuse to follow Prof. Ehrlich in putting their money where their mouths are. Therefore, let's try the chief "official" doomsayer, Vice President Al Gore. He wrote a best-selling book, *Earth in the Balance,* that warns about the supposed environmental and resource "crisis." In my judgment, the book is as ignorant and wrongheaded a collection of clichés as anything ever published on the subject.

CHALLENGE

So how about it, Mr. Vice President? Will you accept my offer? And how about your boss Bill Clinton, who supports your environmental initiatives? Can you bring him in for a piece of the action?

It is not pleasant to talk rudely like this. But a challenge wager is the last refuge of the frustrated. And it is very frustrating that after 25 years of the anti-pessimists being proven entirely right, and the doomsayers being proven entirely wrong, the latter's credibility and influence wax ever greater.

That's the bad news. The good news is that there is every scientific reason to be joyful about the trends in the condition of the Earth, and hopeful for humanity's future, even if we are falsely told the outlook is grim. So happy belated Earth Day.

READING

21

ENVIRONMENTALISM IS AN OCCUPATION FOR THE WEALTHY

E. Calvin Beisner

E. Calvin Beisner is Associate Professor of interdisciplinary studies at Covenant College in Lookout Mountain, Georgia, and co-author of Where Garden Meets Wilderness: Evangelical Entry into Environmental Debate *(Eerdmans, 1997).*

■ POINTS TO CONSIDER

1. What are the macro indicators of poverty which Beisner employs? What are the micro indicators?

2. Why are underdeveloped nations also environmentally degraded, according to the author?

3. Summarize the policy decisions criticized by the author.

4. Assess the statement: "Environmentalism is distinctly a preoccupation of the wealthy."

Beisner, E. Calvin. "How Environmentalism Disdains the Poor." **The Freeman.** August 1998: 461-3. © 1998 The Foundation for Economic Education, Inc.

Environmentalism is distinctly a preoccupation of the wealthy.

The late Julian Simon and other wise thinkers have long understood that economic development is necessary to enable people to afford a safe environment. That insight fits in with my own observations when, several years ago, I attended the Oxford Conference on Christian Faith and Economics at Agra, India – city of the beautiful Taj Mahal. Like many other participants, I was struck by many things: hard-working, friendly, often generous people, each striving to improve life for himself and his family; thousands of charming little children working right alongside their elders in the shops, cottage industries, factories, and streets; beautiful handwoven rugs, tapestries, and clothes; exquisite handmade pottery, some of it produced with the same mosaic techniques that mark the Taj Mahal itself. All of these, and many others, I saw as signs of a society brimming with enterprise. Hopeful signs.

SIGNS OF POVERTY

But in the very same place I saw other signs, the signs of poverty.

Most of the generous people working diligently in the shops and factories, pedaling the rickshaws, or eagerly selling their handmade wares were clearly poor, devastatingly poor. In 1994, India's gross national product per capita was only about a tenth of Latin America's average, and less than one-eightieth that of the United States; its under-five mortality rate was more than twice Latin America's and almost ten times the United States'; and its average life expectancy at birth was 12 percent lower than Latin America's and 20 percent lower than the United States'.

With the Indians' poverty came the visible signs so familiar to anyone who spends time among the poor. Their clothing usually was ill fitting, heavily worn, often repeatedly mended, and more often in need of mending. Despite their honest efforts, the poor Indians usually were not very clean. The tools of their trade were old and inefficient. It was clear that many, even most of them, lived on the streets, the better off among them in little makeshift huts of discarded scrap metal or wood. Almost all looked prematurely aged, their teeth and hands joined by their wrinkled faces in quiet testimony to a hard life.

A BETTER LIFE

As I gazed on the little children scrabbling desperately for a living, I experienced what so many Westerners experience: that longing to take one home – no, to take lots of them home with me, to give them a better life. It is just what some of those children, the orphans, needed. As for those whose parents were living, most, if given the opportunity to trade their poverty with their beloved families for wealth among strangers, would certainly choose their families – and rightly so, for what shall it profit a man if he gain the whole world but lose his own soul?

One sign of the poverty of these people, one that almost every Western environmentalist would completely misunderstand, is the lamentable state of their environment. To call it polluted, for someone accustomed to life in the West, would be the grossest understatement. Indeed, among people gathered for that conference, including Christian missionaries from all over the world, one of the most common observations was that this was the filthiest place we had ever witnessed.

BLIND ACCEPTANCE

Most environmentalists blindly accept Paul Ehrlich's formula that negative environmental impact varies directly in proportion to population, affluence, and technology (I = PAT). But in fact, the wretched environment of Agra, like that of almost all India, is directly rooted in the lack of advanced technologies and wealth.

Indians do not burn dried dung and scrap wood as their chief sources of heat and cooking fuel because they like those better than natural gas and electricity. They do so because their society is too poor to provide the infrastructure without which natural gas and electricity cannot be made available, and the people would be too poor to pay for them – or the furnaces and stoves that would use them – even if they were available. They don't like breathing air filled with the smoke of burning dung, and they would gladly trade that for the smog of moderately advanced industrialized cities if they could afford it – let alone for the clean air of most of the high-income cities of Western Europe, North America, Australia, and Japan, where smog levels have been falling for most of the last three decades.

TOO POOR

But that is just the problem. They can't afford the cleaner environment because they can't afford the technologies that enable people to have a clean environment. And so they, along with hundreds of millions of other poor people in poor countries the world over, suffer the environmental costs of poverty: indoor air pollution from the coarsest biomass fuels, causing respiratory diseases that take millions of lives annually; untreated or minimally treated sewage contaminating surface and subsurface drinking water sources, again taking millions of lives annually; and low-efficiency car and truck engines burning high-lead and high-sulphur fuel, adding to air pollution.

As their economies grow, through continued hard work, learning, and capital investment, those sources of pollution that cost the most in human health and life will diminish. But it will take time, and it won't be easy.

POLICY

Now, how do Western environmentalist leaders respond to these tragedies:

- By insisting, with Vice President Al Gore, that fighting global warming – even the reality of which, let alone the extent and impact, is open to serious debate among climatologists – should be the central organizing principle of human civilization. Although they know that energy use drives economic growth, which replaces poverty with affluence, they insist that fossil fuels be strictly limited.

- By insisting that chlorofluorocarbons, the cheapest and least corrosive of refrigerants, be banned to protect the stratospheric ozone layer from a depletion that remains largely theoretical and that cannot be heavily influenced by the human sources of the ozone-destroying chlorine monoxide, which are dwarfed by nature's sources. They do so even though they know that the ban will delay the time when poor people in poor countries can afford the refrigeration they so desperately need to minimize food spoilage and the malnutrition and food poisoning associated with it.

- And by putting greater emphasis on saving theoretically endangered species before hundreds of millions of people endangered by malnutrition and disease – despite the fact that the International Union for the Conservation of Nature, in a worldwide field survey looking for evidence of rapid species extinctions, could find none.

WEALTHIER IS HEALTHIER

The irony is that Western environmentalist leaders are cutting off the branch on which they sit. Environmentalism is distinctly a preoccupation of the wealthy. Environmental protection increases precisely to the extent that a society becomes wealthy enough to afford it. To the extent they succeed in slowing economic growth anywhere in the world – in rich and poor nations alike – they delay the progress of environmental protection. And while they're at it, they generate a very understandable resentment among the poor of this world, who see these environmentalist leaders as blocking efforts to keep their children from dying or suffering serious, lifelong respiratory ailments. As they alienate the poor, environmentalists also create a mistrust that will delay the time when the poor, ascending out of their poverty – as they surely will – become willing to allocate significant parts of their newfound wealth to environmental protection.

Real friends of the environment recognize that growing economies are the environment's best friends. As economist Indur M. Goklany points out: "The level of affluence at which a pollutant level peaks (or environmental transition occurs) varies. A World Bank analysis concluded that urban airborne particulate matter and sulfur dioxide concentrations peaked at per capita incomes of $3,280 and $3,670, respectively. Fecal coliform bacteria in river water increased with affluence until income reached $1,375 per capita."

REAL FRIENDS

After these peaks, pollutant levels fall off rapidly as wealth continues to increase. This means that real friends of the environment are also real friends of the poor – unlike those who mistakenly believe that economic growth threatens the environment – for they will promote the economic growth that will not only improve the health, life expectancy, and material living standards of the poor but also lead to the cleaner, safer, more sustainable environment they seek.

READING

22

THE WORLD'S POOR SEEK ENVIRONMENTAL JUSTICE

Brian Tokar

Brian Tokar is a member of the Toward Freedom Advisory Board and teaches at the Institute for Social Ecology and Goddard College in Vermont. He is the author of Earth for Sale *(South End Press, 1997) and* The Green Alternative *(New Society Publishers). The following is adapted from* Earth for Sale *and appeared in the journal* Toward Freedom.

■ POINTS TO CONSIDER

1. What criticisms does the author have of the mainstream environmental movement?

2. Define the current paradigm with regard to development.

3. Identify examples of Third World efforts to save the environment.

4. What direction does the author encourage in order to save the environment?

Tokar, Brian. "Beyond the Green Facade." **Toward Freedom.** May 1997: 5-7. Adapted from **Earth for Sale** (South End Press, 1997). Reprinted with permission.

It is vital that we understand how the world looks when one steps outside the boundaries of a Northern industrial, consumerist world-view.

Environmental awareness in the industrialized world is often seen as a product of affluence and economic security. Despite the very real and immediate consequences of air and water pollution, habitat destruction, and the disproportionate siting of toxic industrial facilities in the most impoverished communities, environmental problems are disparaged as an elite concern. Wider international acceptance of an environmental agenda, we're frequently told, will first require the elevation of the world's poor to First World consumption levels. Mainstream environmental groups often unwittingly perpetuate this view by divorcing environmental concerns from their broader social and political context.

The emergence of articulate and occasionally militant Third World voices in the ecology movement during the past decade offers a necessary counterpoint to such myths. In societies where people still live close to the land, its ecological integrity is far from a luxury. For people struggling to sustain traditional ways of life amidst sometimes overwhelming development pressures, maintaining their home region's forests, soils, water, and wildlife is an urgent matter of survival. Third World ecological movements thus complement grassroots eco-activists' efforts in the U.S., and offer an important challenge to the leading mainstream environmental groups. Further, they offer support for the growing understanding that neoliberalism's social and economic dislocations, rather than population growth or "under-development," are the main causes of poverty, malnutrition, social decay, and environmental destruction.

DEFYING DUALISMS

Since the late 1980s, Northern activists have become increasingly aware of Third World peoples' movements struggling to protect traditional lands from the ravages of the global market economy. Indigenous peoples' struggles in the tropical rainforests, from Brazil to Malaysia, first began to alert many Northern environmentalists to the importance of an internationalist perspective. The dramatic actions of peoples such as the Yanomami and the Penan, who regularly risk their lives to resist the incursions of multinational timber interests, are sometimes reported even in mainstream media.

Another movement that's gained widespread attention is the Chipko, or tree-hugging, movement, initiated by indigenous women of northern India's highlands in the 1970s. Merging traditional Hindu devotion to forest integrity with the more recent tradition of Gandhian nonviolence, the Chipko women and men have intervened against native forest exploitation and displacement of indigenous ecosystems by plantations of commercially valued trees. Fasting, embracing ancient trees, lying down before logging trucks, and removing planted eucalyptus seedlings that strain precious groundwater supplies, the Chipko people have asserted that forests' role in replenishing the soil, water, and air must take precedence over their exploitation as a source of exotic exported timber.

Larry Lohmann of *The Ecologist* magazine, who spent many years living and working in Thailand, has highlighted such movements' uniqueness and diversity. They're rarely simply "environmental," but emerge from a complex interplay of social, political, cultural, historical, and ecological factors and usually defy Western dualisms of public v. private ownership, morality v. self interest, biocentrism v. anthropocentrism, militancy v. pragmatism. They tend to emerge from people's determination to sustain traditional communal systems of livelihood, production, and allocation, rooted in distinct cultural and social patterns, from Western development's intolerably destabilizing pressures. These movements emerge, says Lohmann, from "the democratically evolving practices of ordinary people."

DAILY URGENCY

The North's "free-trade" policies, often viewed in remote, statistical terms by Northern activists, are also a matter of daily urgency to many Third World peoples. For example, farmers in India have developed a militant movement against corporate control of agriculture. Under the guise of fighting hunger, corporate agribusiness has heightened social inequality in many of the world's agricultural regions and made people increasingly dependent on the corporate-dominated global economy. At the same time, industrial farming methods lower groundwater levels, poison the land with chemicals, and undermine the species diversity that has long sustained indigenous agricultures.

Farmers in the southwestern Indian state of Karnataka have focused on the increasing dominance of Cargill and other transnational corporations and the threat they pose to land, water, and food security. In 1992, activists entered Cargill's regional office in Bangalore, removed records and supplies of seeds and tossed them into a bonfire, reminiscent of British textile burnings during India's independence movement. The following summer, 200 members of the state's peasant organization dismantled Cargill's regional seed storage unit and razed it. In October 1993, half a million farmers joined a day-long rally in Bangalore to protest corporate control of agriculture, patenting of seeds and other life forms, and new trade and patent rules required by the then-proposed General Agreement on Tariffs and Trade (GATT) agreement. Their demands included a strong affirmation of the tradition of free cultivation and seed exchange by India's farmers, a tradition that's threatened by the global regime of "intellectual property rights."

POPULATION

Such movements stand in sharp contrast to images of helpless Third World peoples we usually see in the mainstream press, images reinforced by many mainstream environmentalists' singular focus on population growth. The population issue is exploited by those who would sever the fundamental link between ecology and social justice. For example, the World Wildlife Fund described the world's poor in the late 1980s as the "most direct threat to wildlife and wildlands." Population concerns have largely become a smokescreen to obscure the patterns of colonialism and exploitation that are primarily responsible for destruction of the South's ecological integrity. Discussions of over-population invariably focus on countries in Africa and southern Asia, rather than Holland, for instance, which probably has the world's highest population density, or Japan, which imports much of its food, timber, and other necessities. Third World population growth cannot be dismissed as a matter of ecological concern, but it's a symptom, not a cause, of environmental and social degradation.

THE CURRENT PARADIGM

Even those institutions most responsible for the present state of affairs are being pressed to acknowledge who's really overconsuming the earth's resources. The World Bank has helped drive countless countries into debilitating cycles of poverty and dependency in the name of "structural adjustment": the reorientation of the world's economies toward debt repayment, privatization of public services and promotion of foreign investment. However, even the Bank is compelled to acknowledge that industrialized countries, with barely 20 percent of the world's population, consume well over 80 percent of the goods. Between 1900 and 1990, the world's human population tripled, but fossil fuel use increased 30 times and industrial output increased fifty-fold. A more graphic example is cited by Malaysian activist Martin Khor, who decries the "gross inequalities in the use of natural resources epitomized by the fact that New Yorkers use more energy commuting in a week than the energy used by all Africans for all uses in a year." There is nothing inevitable about the relationship between population and consumption, especially when considered in regionally-specific terms.

Still, many mainstream environmentalists endorse the view that development is the answer to inequality, even if it's carried out with only a veneer of environmental sustainability. For many Third World activists, this is merely the latest incarnation of the 500-year legacy of European colonialism. As Muto Ichiyo, of the Tokyo-based Pacific-Asia Resource Center describes it, "Economic development, which was supposed to raise the world out of poverty, has so far only transformed undeveloped poverty into developed modernized poverty designed to function smoothly in the world economic system." It brings toxic hazards, such as Bhopal and sweatshop industries that assault people's health and well being.

MAINSTREAM

One particularly insidious expression of the current development paradigm has been some U.S.-based environmental groups' active participation in government-funded international development efforts. Assistance ostensibly designed to encourage environmental technologies is often used as a wedge to satisfy transnational capital's needs. A recent report by the U.S. Agency for International Development (AID) advocated "the forging of environmental policies to favor private sector, market-based solutions ... and supporting market-based approaches to biodiversity preservation and enhancement. Technical assistance to address environmental problems is often tied to enactment of measures limiting foreign investors' liability for environmental damages. In 1993, $132 million in such assistance was funded by AID and channeled through environmental organizations such as the

World Wildlife Fund, Nature Conservancy, Conservation International, and the World Resources Institute, according to Tom Barry of the Interhemispheric Resource Center.

As India's Vandana Shiva often points out, development does much more than perpetuate poverty and sustain the institutions of Northern domination. It systematically degrades the knowledge, skills, and cultural practices that made it possible for people to thrive outside of a commercial context for thousands of years. In India, development turns once self-reliant farmers into "credit addicts and chemical addicts"; in Africa, it turns indigenous pastoralists into beggars at elite safari camps; and even in the West, in northern Quebec's boreal forests, it has meant the relocation of many recently intact Cree villages into prefabricated neighborhoods entirely dependent on imported consumer goods. Once relocated into the global market, people invariably confront the same debilitating social ills that affect urbanized and suburban peoples throughout the world.

DEVELOPMENT ALTERNATIVES

In the late 1980s and early 90s, the concept of "sustainable development" became widely accepted as an agenda for reconciling environmental protection with economic development. The term emerged from UN studies and commissions, culminating in the widely quoted 1988 Brundtland Commission report, *Our Common Future,* and the 1992 UN "Earth Summit" in Rio de Janeiro. While the Rio conference made "sustainable development" a household term among mainstream environmentalists, and helped enshrine it as the official policy of governmental agencies throughout the world, many activists in the North and South see it as a fundamental contradiction in terms.

For most of these governments, and many international agencies, the project of making development environmentally sustainable has been transformed into one of sustaining development and economic growth. Clearly, the earth's ecosystems cannot possibly survive the five- to ten-fold increase in economic activity predicted by sustainable development advocates. Two hundred years of Northern industrial development occurred largely at the expense of the South's lands, resources, and people. Where will the emerging middle classes of the developing world's cities find the equivalent resources to appropriate in development's name? What promise does this development offer to the tens of millions

© 1990 Joel Pett, **Lexington Herald - Leader**

of people who've been forced off the land and into the maelstrom of the global cash economy?

Realizing the long-range impossibility – and immediate social and ecological consequences – of the Western model of development, Third World ecologists and traditional peoples are seeking a different kind of vision for the future, embracing indigenous traditions and rejecting the mythical benefits of replacing subsistence-based economies with the buying and selling of commodified goods. Campaigns to resist intrusions of the market economy against traditional lands and economic practices are rarely reported in the official international press, but such efforts are becoming more organized and politically conscious.

Farmers from Ecuador to West Africa to the Philippines are returning to traditional farming methods and banning the use of chemicals and modern machinery in traditional territories. Fishing communities in India and the Philippines have established coastal zones from which mechanized commercial fishing boats are banned. Malaysian activists forced the cancellation of a five billion dollars mega-dam project that would have displaced 9000 people and become the world's second largest.

BEYOND CONSUMERISM

A landless peoples' movement in Brazil has occupied traditional

ENVIRONMENTAL RACISM

The environmental theme was to sound repeatedly in civil rights struggles long before environmental justice emerged as a movement unto itself. Indeed, it was a garbage strike that brought Martin Luther King, Jr., to Memphis in 1968, where he was assassinated. King's mission was to assist garbage workers protesting their unequal pay and unsafe working conditions....

Robert D. Bullard. "The Environmental Justice Movement Comes of Age." **The Amicus Journal.** Spring 1994: 32-7.

lands, rejecting the control of absentee landowners committed to raising cash crops, and people throughout southern Mexico, inspired by the Zapatista rebels of Chiapas, are defying the corrupt political oligarchy that's dominated that country for nearly 70 years. The Zapatista rebellion of January 1994 coincided with North American Free Trade Agreement's (NAFTA) enactment and pledged to reverse the Mexican government's abolition of constitutionally guaranteed communal land rights. One town in central Mexico expelled officials who supported the construction of luxury hotels, condominiums, and a golf course on indigenous lands, and declared a "free municipality" independent of the state government.

With industrialized societies' inequalities in wealth and power beginning to parallel the huge disparities between North and South, it is clear that the ecological crisis cannot be addressed without seriously confronting the underlying causes of poverty and inequality. It is vital that we understand how the world looks when one steps outside the boundaries of a Northern industrial, consumerist world-view. The traditional knowledge of indigenous peoples and the social and economic analysis of Third World activists are helping to unmask the green facade of neocolonialism and challenge the political complacency of many Northern environmentalists. This challenge has become especially urgent as mainstream environmental groups help legitimize the use of environmental rhetoric by the U.S. government, the World Bank, and other global institutions.

"Given the key role they are fated to play in the politics of an ever-shrinking world," Tom Athanasiou writes in his pioneering book, *Divided Planet,* "it is past time for environmentalists to face their own history." Environmentalists have become advocates, sometimes unwittingly, "merely for the comforts and aesthetics of affluent nature lovers," Athanasiou continues. Today this is no longer tolerable. "They have no choice. History will judge greens by whether they stand with the world's poor." To adopt such a stance and heed the messages of Third World ecologists may ultimately help us discover what is most sustainable in our own diverse cultures as well.

WHAT IS EDITORIAL BIAS?

This activity may be used as an individualized study guide for students in libraries and resource centers or as a discussion catalyst in small group and classroom discussions.

The capacity to recognize an author's point of view is an essential reading skill. The skill to read with insight and understanding involves the ability to detect different kinds of opinions or bias. Sex bias, race bias, ethnocentric bias, political bias, and religious bias are five basic kinds of opinions expressed in editorials and all literature that attempts to persuade. They are briefly defined below.

Five Kinds of Editorial Opinion or Bias

Sex Bias — The expression of dislike for and/or feeling of superiority over a person because of gender or sexual preference.

Race Bias — The expression of dislike for and/or feeling of superiority over a racial group.

Ethnocentric Bias — The expression of a belief that one's own group, race, religion, culture, or nation is superior. Ethnocentric persons judge others by their own standards and values.

Political Bias — The expression of political opinions and attitudes about government-related issues on the local, state, national or international level.

Religious Bias — The expression of a religious belief or attitude.

Guidelines

1. From the readings in Chapter Three, locate five sentences that provide examples of editorial opinion or bias.

2. Write down each of the above sentences and determine what kind of bias each sentence represents. Is it **sex bias, race bias, ethnocentric bias, political bias** or **religious bias**?

3. Make up one-sentence statements that would be an example of each of the following: **sex bias, race bias, ethnocentric bias, political bias** and **religious bias.**

4. See if you can locate five sentences that are factual statements from the readings in Chapter Three.

BIBLIOGRAPHY

Book References

An Agenda to Address Climate Change. ed. Natural Resources Canada. Ottawa: Natural Resources Canada, 1998.

Bromley, Daniel W. **Environment and Economy: Property Rights and Public Policy.** Cambridge, MA: B. Blackwell, 1991.

Brown, Lester R., et al. **Beyond Malthus: Sixteen Dimensions of the Population Problem.** Washington, D.C.: Worldwatch Institute, 1998.

Climate Change 1995: Economic and Social Dimensions of Climate Change. ed. James P. Bruce, Hoesung Lee, Erik R. Haites. New York: Published for The Intergovernmental Panel on Climate Change, Cambridge University Press, 1996.

Climate Change 1995: The Science of Climate Change. ed. J.T. Houghton, et al. New York: Published for The Intergovernmental Panel on Climate Change, Cambridge University Press, 1996.

Economics and Policy Issues in Climate Change. ed. William D. Nordhaus. Washington, D.C.: Resources for the Future, 1998.

The Economics of Population: Classic Writings. ed. Julian Simon. New Brunswick: Transaction Publishers, 1998.

Fletcher, Susan R. **Global Climate Change Treaty: The Kyoto Protocol.** Washington, D.C.: Congressional Research Service, 1998.

A Guide to Understanding the National Environmental Policy Act: Created to Safeguard the Nation's Environment. Alexandria, VA: National Guard Bureau, Environment and Public Affairs, 1998.

Jepma, C.J. **Climate Change and Policy: Facts, Issues, Analysis.** New York: Cambridge University Press, 1998.

Moore, Thomas Gale. **Climate of Fear: Why We Shouldn't Worry about Global Warming.** Washington, D.C.: Cato Institute, 1998.

Oceans: Into the Next Millennium of Oceanographic Research. Developed for Discussion during 1998, The Year of the Oceans. Washington, D.C.: National Oceanic and Atmospheric Administration, 1998.

Our Ocean Future: Themes and Issues Concerning the Nation's Stake in the Oceans. Developed for Discussion during 1998, The Year of the Oceans. Washington, D.C.: National Oceanic and Atmospheric Administration, 1998.

Parker, Larry. **Global Climate Change: Market-Based Strategies to Reduce Greenhouse Gases.** Washington, D.C.: Congressional Research Services, 1998.

Property Rights and the Environment: Social and Ecological Issues. ed. Susan Hanna and Mohan Munasinghe. Washington, D.C.: Beijer Institute of Ecological Economics and the World Bank, 1995.

The Road Back: Endangered Species Recovery Success with Partners. Washington, D.C.: U.S. Department of the Interior, U.S. Fish and Wildlife Service, 1998.

Rosenzweig, Cynthia. **Climate Change and the Global Harvest: Potential Impacts of the Greenhouse Effect on Agriculture.** New York: Oxford University Press, 1998.

State of the World. ed. Lisa Starke. New York: Worldwatch Institute, 1998.

Switzer, Jacqueline Vaughn. **Environmental Politics: Domestic and Global Dimensions,** 2d Ed. New York: St. Martin's Press, 1998.

Voluntary Agreements with Industry. ed. Organization for Economic Co-operation and Development. Washington, D.C.: OECD Publications and Information Center, 1998.

Journal References

"After Kyoto: The Cost of Cutting Greenhouse Gas Emissions." **Engineering & Mining Journal.** October 1998.

Baker, Beth. "1998 – The Year of the Ocean." **BioScience.** April 1998.

Bethell, Tom. "Losing One's Soul Facing Up to the Spiritual Hazards of Wealth." **The American Spectator.** November 1998.

Bowler, Sue. "Recycling the Earth." **New Scientist.** January 17, 1998.

Browne, E.J.P. "Energy Companies and the Environment Can Coexist." **USA Today Magazine.** September 1998.

Burke, Tom. "There's a Long, Hard Slog Ahead: International Cooperation on Environmental Protection." **New Statesman.** September 25, 1998.

Cane, Mark A. "A Role for the Tropical Pacific." **Science.** October 2, 1998.

Dasgupta, Partha and Gretchen Daily. "Food Production, Population Growth, and the Environment." **Science.** August 28, 1998.

Dawson, P.J. and Richard Tiffin. "Is There a Long-Run Relationship between Population Growth and Living Standards?" **Journal of Development Studies.** June 1998.

Forsyth, Tim. "Technology Transfer and the Climate Change Debate." **Environment.** November 1998.

Gerholm, Tor Ragnar. "The Atomic Age Is Not Over Yet: Nuclear Power and Environmental Protection." **New Statesman.** September 25, 1998.

Goldstein, Edward. "Waterworld." **Government Executive.** April 1998.

Hallowell, Christopher. "Save the Swordfish: An Alliance of Chefs and Conservationists Wants You to Forgo a Delicacy." **Time.** January 26, 1998.

Hanson, Gayle M.B. "Mr. Gore's Wild Warming Theory." **Insight on the News.** August 31, 1998.

Harad, George. "The Kyoto Climate Control Protocol." **Pulp and Paper.** November 1, 1998.

Hollingsworth, William G. "Population Explosion: Still Expanding." **USA Today Magazine.** July 1998.

Lee, Michael et al. "Growth Convergence: Some Panel Data Evidence." **Applied Economics.** July 1998.

Leland, Ted. "Global Warming: Political Hot Potato Warrants Comprehensive Approach." **Appliance Manufacturer.** October 1, 1998.

Music, Kimberley. "Industry Supports Oceans Bill Despite Its New Bureaucracy." **The Oil Daily.** March 19, 1998.

Menon, Subhadra. "Climate Change: Heating Up, Flooded Out." **India Today.** October 5, 1998.

Mulvaney, Kieran. "Hot Air Over Cold Climes." **New Scientist.** September 1998.

Mulvaney, Kieran. "A Sea of Troubles." **E.** January 11, 1998.

Parris, Thomas M. "A Look at Climate Change Skeptics." **Environment.** November 1998.

Pimentel, David et al. "Ecology of Increasing Disease: Population Growth and Environmental Degradation." **BioScience.** October, 1998.

Poster, Sandra L. "Water for Food Production: Will There Be Enough in 2025." **BioScience.** August 1998.

Reiger, George. "Two to Remember: Conservationists Sigurd Olson and Aldo Leopold." **Field & Stream.** July 1998.

Scott, Alex. "BP Experiments with Carbon Dioxide Emissions Trading." **Chemical Week.** October 28, 1998.

Smith, Heather A. "Stopped Cold: Canadian Climate Change Efforts." **Alternatives Journal.** September 22, 1998.

Stagliano, Vito. "Climate Change: The Kyoto Blunder." **Electricity Journal.** October 1998.

Steig, E.J. "Synchronous Climate Changes in Antarctica and the North Atlantic." **Science.** October 2, 1998.

Stocker, Thomas F. "The Seasaw Effect: Rapid and Millennial-scale Climate Change." **Science.** October 2, 1998.

Tomic, Igor. "Land Loss and Erosion in China: A Report." **Review of Business.** December 22, 1998.

"Vietnam-Ocean Environment Deteriorating." **Vietnam Economic News.** July 20, 1998.

Wagner, Cynthia. "Slowing Population Growth in Ireland, Africa." **The Futurist.** November 1998.

"Water Availability and Use." **Economic Review.** September 1998.

Watkins, James D. "On the Crest of a New Ocean Agenda: International Year of the Ocean Heralds New Era of Ocean Science." **Science.** July 1998.

Windridge, Kenneth. "Getting Out of a Fix: Nitrogen Saturation and Agricultural Productivity." **Chemistry and Industry.** October 19, 1998.

"The Year of the Ocean." **Newsweek.** April 13, 1998.

INDEX